INTRODUCING
Philosophy

Dave Robinson • Judy Groves

Edited by Richard Appignanesi

Icon Books UK Totem Books USA

This edition published in the UK
in 2004 by Icon Books Ltd.,
The Old Dairy, Brook Road,
Thriplow, Cambridge SG8 7RG
email: info@iconbooks.co.uk
www.introducingbooks.com

Sold in the UK, Europe, South Africa
and Asia by Faber and Faber Ltd.,
3 Queen Square, London WC1N 3AU
or their agents

Distributed in the UK, Europe, South
Africa and Asia by TBS Ltd., TBS
Distribution Centre, Colchester Road,
Frating Green, Colchester CO7 7DW

This edition published in Australia
in 2004 by Allen & Unwin Pty. Ltd.,
PO Box 8500, 83 Alexander Street,
Crows Nest, NSW 2065

Previously published in the UK
and Australia in 1998 as *Philosophy for
Beginners* and in 1999 as
Introducing Philosophy

Reprinted 1999, 2000, 2001, 2002,
2003, 2005, 2007

This edition published in the USA
in 2004 by Totem Books
Inquiries to Icon Books Ltd.,
The Old Dairy, Brook Road,
Thriplow, Cambridge
SG8 7RG, UK

Distributed to the trade in the USA by
National Book Network Inc.,
4501 Forbes Boulevard, Suite 200,
Lanham, Maryland 20706

Distributed in Canada by
Penguin Books Canada,
90 Eglinton Avenue East, Suite 700,
Toronto, Ontario M4P 2YE

ISBN 978-1840465-76-1

Originating editor: Richard Appignanesi

Printed by Gutenberg Press, Malta

QUESTIONS

Most people are usually too busy to go in for the sort of thinking usually called "philosophical". This is because they have to spend their time struggling for existence or because they rather enjoy living lives of undisturbed routine. But, on rare occasions, a few awkward and irritating individuals with time on their hands ask deceptively simple questions which never seem to have simple answers.

WHAT IS THE NATURE OF REALITY? WHAT ARE HUMAN BEINGS REALLY LIKE?
WHAT IS SPECIAL ABOUT HUMAN MINDS AND CONSCIOUSNESS?
CAN WE BE CERTAIN ABOUT ANYTHING AT ALL?
ARE THERE OBVIOUS DIFFERENCES BETWEEN VALID AND IMPROPER ARGUMENTS?
WHAT IS TRUTH? WHAT IS MEANING?
HOW SHOULD WE BEHAVE TOWARDS EACH OTHER AND HOW SHOULD WE
ORGANIZE SOCIETY? ARE GOVERNMENTS A GOOD IDEA?

WHAT IS PHILOSOPHY?

Questions of philosophy might not appear to have much to do with everyday survival. But philosophers still look for convincing answers. Sometimes they get them, often they don't.

BUT THE QUESTIONS, ONCE ASKED, SEEM NEVER TO GO AWAY.

ORIGINALLY, "PHILOSOPHERS" WERE JUST INDIVIDUALS WHO ASKED QUESTIONS ABOUT EVERYTHING.

NOWADAYS, PHILOSOPHY TENDS TO GET CLASSIFIED MORE RIGOROUSLY.

Epistemology
(questions about knowledge)

Metaphysics
(Time, Space, God, Cause, and Reality)

Ethics
(Good and Bad)

Aesthetics
(Art and Beauty)

Political Philosophy

Some philosophers believe that philosophy must evolve out of *argument* and *debate*, others that it can only ever be produced from *deductive reasoning*.

SOME PHILOSOPHERS BELIEVE THAT PHILOSOPHY CAN MAKE REAL PROGRESS IN THE HUNT FOR KNOWLEDGE.

OTHERS SAY THAT IT IS "THINKING ABOUT THINKING" AND DOES NO MORE THAN HELP TO CLARIFY IDEAS AND REMOVE MISUNDERSTANDINGS.

But all of them believe that philosophers are obliged to provide some kind of explanation, proof or evidence for their ideas. And this obligation marks the one obvious difference between philosophy and religion.

THEOCRACIES

The Ancient Egyptians were very good at maths and at building geometric tombs, but they're not famous for philosophy. Their religious explanations of things are elaborate and colourful but unconvincing in philosophical terms. The Babylonians were likewise wonderful mathematicians and astronomers.

> BUT THEY TOO APPEAR SATISFIED WITH MYTHICAL ANSWERS TO FUNDAMENTAL QUESTIONS.

Theocratic societies governed by priestly castes are usually static and monopolize thought. They insist on orthodox explanations and actively discourage independent and unconventional ideas. Today's beliefs must always be like yesterday's.

THE GREEKS

The Ancient Greeks invented philosophy, but no-one really knows why. The Greeks were a great trading nation who dominated much of the eastern Mediterranean and borrowed myths and mysticism as well as architecture and mathematics from their neighbours. But some worrisome Greek philosopher-scientists thought there just had to be some kind of underlying order or logic for the way things are. They were not willing to accept religious explanations – for instance, thinkers like **Xenophanes** (c. 560-478 B.C.).

IT IS NAIVE TO WORSHIP THE GODS BECAUSE THEY ALL BEHAVE IRRATIONALLY AND IMMORALLY.

IF HORSES HAD HANDS AND COULD DRAW, THEY WOULD DRAW PICTURES OF GODS LIKE HORSES.

So the first Greek philosophers looked for answers which we would now call "scientific" rather than "religious".

7

THE MILESIANS' BIG QUESTION

The first real philosophers were some eccentric Greeks who lived in Miletus, a colony on what is now the Turkish coast, in the 6th century B.C. They asked **The One Big Question** – what is reality made of? Actually, it's a very strange question to ask. Most people would say that the world is made up of lots of different things, because it looks that way. But these Milesians didn't accept that what you **see** is necessarily the same as what is **true**.

Anaximander also thought that the earth was like a large stone column. Not much is known about any of these strange early philosopher-scientists, except that their science was almost wholly cerebral and not experimental. But they would never accept answers which relied merely on supernatural explanations.

PYTHAGORAS AND MATHEMATICS

Pythagoras (571-496 B.C.) asked the same One Big Question, but emerged with a very different answer. He thought that the answer was *mathematics*. He lived on the island of Samos, before he emigrated with his disciples to Croton in southern Italy. He was a vegetarian who believed in reincarnation and declared that eating beans was sinful. He and his disciples worshipped numbers and thought that the world was made of them, a truth most obviously revealed by ratios, squares and right-angled triangles. Pythagoras' big breakthrough was to recognize that mathematical truths had to be proved rather than just accepted. His number mysticism looks to us very odd. He declared that "Justice" was the number 4, because it was a square number. He was finally shocked by his discovery of "irrational" numbers like Pi and √2.

THE RATIO OF THE CIRCUMFERENCE OF A CIRCLE TO ITS DIAMETER IS – APPROXIMATELY 3.141 ...

APPROXIMATELY? THIS SUGGESTS THAT THE WORLD ISN'T AT ALL MATHEMATICALLY NEAT AND PERFECT.

He even drowned one of his students, Hipparsus of Tarentum, for revealing this awkward truth to outsiders. So not all philosophers are broad-minded about student debate.

HERACLITUS AND THE WORLD IN FLUX

Heraclitus, who lived circa 500 B.C., would have been more tolerant of an irrational universe. His nickname was "The Rudder" because he maintained that everything in the world is always changing and in a constant state of conflict. He illustrated this by a famous saying.

YOU CAN NEVER STEP INTO THE SAME RIVER TWICE.

Cratylus (c. 400 B.C.), his student, went further.

YOU CAN'T STEP INTO THE SAME RIVER EVEN *ONCE*.

But Heraclitus is often misunderstood: his view of the universe is really one of underlying unity and consistency. The knowledge that we get from our senses, and foolishly believe in, is inevitably "observer-relative".

A mountain goes both up or down depending on where you are standing at the time. But that's what mountains do.

THE PATH UP AND THE PATH DOWN IS ONE AND THE SAME.

If a river didn't change all the time, it wouldn't be a river. But nevertheless, we still know that's what it is. So Heraclitus may have been suggesting that true knowledge comes from thinking with the mind, not from looking at things. His emphasis on accelerated change may also be why his contribution to the One Big Question was that the world was ultimately made of fire – something that is always changing and yet still uniquely itself.

PARMENIDES

Parmenides of Elea (515-450 B.C.) in southern Italy wrote a long poem about the power of logic and knowledge. He agreed with Heraclitus that empirical knowledge was unreliably subjective. This meant that human beings had only reason to rely on if they wanted to discover any permanent truths about the world.

> FOR IT IS THE SAME THING TO THINK AND TO BE.

By employing strict logical argument he produced an interesting idea about Time: all that actually exists is the immediate present. Talk about the past and the future is just talk – neither has any real existence. Parmenides is still rather admired by philosophers because he was always prepared to accept any conclusions produced by rigorous deductive argument, however odd they might seem.

ZENO'S PARADOX OF MOTION

His student **Zeno** (490-430 B.C.) is famous for inventing paradoxes which explore the often puzzling relationships that exist between space and time. The most famous concerns a race between Achilles and a tortoise. Achilles sportingly gives the tortoise a head start which is proportionate to his slowness. But Achilles finds that he can never reach his reptilian opponent.

IF ACHILLES IS TO GET FROM A TO THE FINISHING POST B, HE MUST FIRST REACH POINT C, THE STARTING-POINT OF THE TORTOISE.

BUT BY THIS TIME THE TORTOISE WILL HAVE MOVED TO POINT D, AND WHEN ACHILLES GETS THERE, FRUSTRATINGLY, THE TORTOISE WILL HAVE MOVED TO POINT E, AND SO ON ...

The tortoise will always be a little bit ahead of Achilles, and is uncatchable. It's an argument that still worries some philosophers, mathematicians and physicists. There is also a point to these puzzles. Zeno is suggesting that real motion and change are impossible – the view held by his master Parmenides.

EMPEDOCLES AND THE FOUR ELEMENTS

Empedocles (490-430 B.C.) lived in the Greek colony of Sicily. He was a doctor who produced his own answer to the One Big Question.

THE WORLD IS MADE OF EARTH, AIR, FIRE AND WATER. IT IS RULED BY THE TWO FORCES OF LOVE AND STRIFE, OR ATTRACTION AND REPULSION.

THE FOUR ELEMENTS WERE HELD TO BE THE BASIC SUBSTANCES UNTIL MEDIEVAL TIMES.

Introducing these new forces was a new attempt to explain how compounds are made and destroyed. His physics may have led him to believe in a constant cycle of destructive and constructive reincarnation. He claimed to have already been "a boy and a girl, a bush and a bird and a sea-fish" before he became Empedocles. He ended his life by jumping into the Mount Etna volcano, perhaps as a demonstration of his philosophy.

THE ATOMISTS

Anaxagoras (500-428 B.C.) explained how it is that you are what you eat. Everything is a mixture. So there are portions of blood, flesh, bone, hair and nails in wheat, which explains how food makes human bodies.

ULTIMATELY, THERE IS A PIECE OF EVERYTHING IN EVERYTHING ELSE, AND EVERYTHING THEREFORE CONSISTS OF AN INFINITE NUMBER OF SMALL THINGS.

THERE MUST BE TINY THINGS THAT FINALLY CANNOT BE "CUT" ANY FURTHER, OTHERWISE MATTER COULD NOT EXIST. THESE "UNCUTTABLES" OR "ATOMS" MOVE, COLLIDE, FORM NEW COMPOUNDS AND ARE INDIVISIBLE, ALL OF WHICH EXPLAINS THE OBJECTIVE QUALITIES OF THE WORLD LIKE WEIGHT, SHAPE AND SIZE.

OTHER QUALITIES LIKE SMELL ONLY COME INTO BEING WHEN THE ATOMS OF AN OBJECT INTERACT WITH THE ATOMS OF THE HUMAN NOSE.

Democritus the Atomist (460-370 B.C.) was a contemporary of Socrates and is famous for his conjectural views about matter which startlingly anticipate the theories of 20th century atomic physicists.

INTRODUCING SOCRATES

All these theories of mind and the ultimate nature of the world are known as "pre-Socratic". What is remarkable about these conjectures is how close some of them got to 20th century scientific theory. They got to this stage, not by using particle accelerators, but just by thinking very hard.

Socrates (470-399 B.C.) lived in 5th century B.C. Athens, a small "city-state" with a powerful Mediterranean empire. Many Athenians were slave-owners, which gave them plenty of leisure time in which to invent things like drama, history, astronomy and philosophy. They thought they were the most civilized nation on earth, and they probably were.

CULTURAL RELATIVISM

Herodotus (484-424 B.C.) the historian had travelled extensively beyond Greece and made some startling discoveries about the beliefs and behaviour of other societies. Sophist philosophers like **Protagoras** (490-420 B.C.) saw the full implications of this. It led him to ask some worrying questions.

> IF OTHER PEOPLE BELIEVE IN DIFFERENT THINGS TO YOU, HOW DO YOU KNOW THAT YOUR BELIEFS ARE RIGHT? HOW DO YOU KNOW THAT ANYONE'S BELIEFS ARE RIGHT?

It's always easy to believe that your beliefs are "natural" when they are only "cultural". So, the Sophists changed the subject of philosophical investigation from the One Big Question to different ones about human beings and their societies.

17

PROTAGORAS THE SOPHIST

Protagoras said that "Man is the measure of all things" – which means that there are no objective truths, only limited human beliefs. This makes him sound very relativist and even postmodern. He also claimed that philosophy was really no more than rhetoric or the art of verbal persuasion (a useful skill to have in debates) and that learning this skill made his students "good men".

WE ARE CALLED "SOPHISTS" BECAUSE WE ARE PAID TO TEACH THIS SKILL OF WISDOM.

AND THAT'S WHY WE HAVE **SOPHISTRY**! YOU ANNOY ME NO END. THERE'S A LOT MORE TO PHILOSOPHY THAN VERBAL TRICKS.

Socrates was a small, scruffy and ugly little man with a snub nose. His father was a stonemason and his mother a midwife. His own wife Xantippe sold vegetables and often found her husband infuriatingly vague. But he was clearly a kind of charismatic guru for many young Athenians, perhaps because he taught them to question **everything** – an odd habit which no doubt irritated their parents.

SOCRATIC DIALOGUE

Socrates always claimed that he knew nothing, which is why the Delphic oracle called him "the wisest man in Greece". He actively encouraged his students to argue about ideas, usually to show them how hard it is to produce satisfactory answers to philosophical questions. The uncertainty that this irritating "Socratic dialogue" produced in people's minds may explain why Socrates' nickname was "the Gadfly".

KNOW THYSELF.

Nobody knows whether he genuinely believed that philosophical dialogue could discover the ultimate truths about concepts like "Justice" so that they could then be applied to specific moral and political problems. His central belief was that true moral wisdom lay in the self, that "Virtue is knowledge".

CONDEMNED TO DEATH

Unfortunately, Socrates had some dubious friends like Critias who systematically executed many Athenians who disagreed with the rule of the "Thirty Tyrants". When they were finally overthrown, a jury of Democrats took their revenge and the Gadfly was found guilty of impiety and corrupting young Athenians, and so condemned to death. He bravely swallowed hemlock poison after explaining his beliefs to his friends and disciples.

MY LAST WORDS TO YOU ARE ON THE IMMORTALITY OF THE SOUL – SO I AM NOT FEARFUL OF LEAVING THIS WORLD.

Socrates remains an ambiguous figure – a man who had bad taste in political allies, yet always defended the independent thinker against state morality. But he did change philosophy. Philosophical questions were now about human morality and politics, not about the innermost nature of the physical world.

PLATO AND THE PHILOSOPHER KINGS

Plato (427-347 B.C.) was one of Socrates' disciples, but, unlike his teacher, he was an instinctive authoritarian. He was an Athenian aristocrat and hated the Democrats who had condemned Socrates to death.

> *WHEN I OBSERVED ALL THIS ... I WITHDREW IN DISGUST FROM THE ABUSES OF THOSE DAYS.*

He thought his fellow Athenians were becoming soft and decadent, and admired the ruthless militaristic Spartans who kept winning all the wars they fought against Athens. He eventually became a tutor to the son of Dionysius I of Sicily, a very reluctant student, and then returned to Athens to found his **Academy**. His most famous work is **The Republic**, which is his detailed blueprint for a harmonious and thus perfect society ruled over by wise philosopher-rulers.

THE DOCTRINE OF INNATISM

Plato enshrined the Socratic dialogue by writing his philosophy in this form. In his early writings, Plato gave respectability to the doctrine of **Innatism** – the belief that we are all born programmed with certain kinds of knowledge. He demonstrated this by questioning a young slave belonging to his friend Meno.

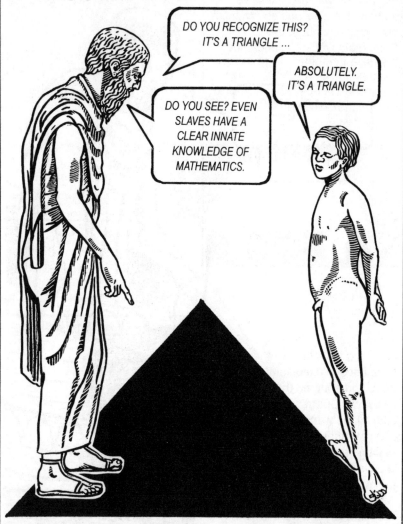

DO YOU RECOGNIZE THIS? IT'S A TRIANGLE ...

ABSOLUTELY. IT'S A TRIANGLE.

DO YOU SEE? EVEN SLAVES HAVE A CLEAR INNATE KNOWLEDGE OF MATHEMATICS.

His explanation for this is that we all possess immortal souls which have had a previous existence, so that all learning is really just "recollection", or *anamnesis*.

THE IDEAL FORMS

This "recollected" view of knowledge helped to make Plato a "two world" man. Although there is the obvious and ordinary everyday world we can all see, there is also another one of eternal perfect "Forms". Forms are like perfect templates, so particular things like chairs that we all see in this world are just inferior copies of the pure or ideal Form of "Chairness". Only a few specially gifted and trained people whom he called "Guardians" can ever "see" these ideal Forms. Not everyone agreed with this.

I CAN SEE A TABLE AND A CUP. I CAN'T SEE TABLENESS AND CUPNESS!

PRECISELY. TO SEE A TABLE AND A CUP YOU NEED EYES, AND YOU HAVE THOSE. TO SEE TABLENESS AND CUPNESS, YOU NEED INTELLIGENCE, AND YOU DON'T HAVE THAT.

THE PARABLE OF THE CAVE

Plato explains his doctrine with a fable. Ordinary people are like prisoners permanently trapped in a dark cave and forced to watch a shadow puppet play which they think is "real".

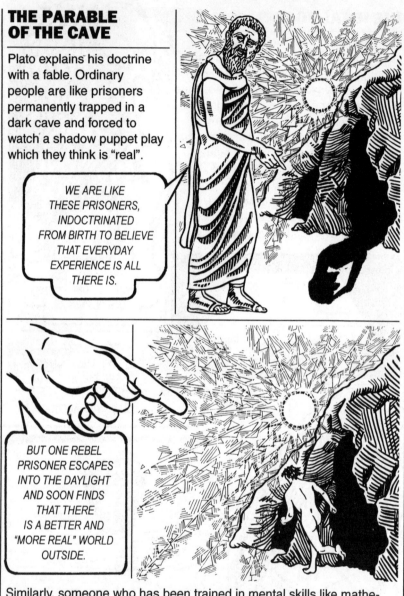

WE ARE LIKE THESE PRISONERS, INDOCTRINATED FROM BIRTH TO BELIEVE THAT EVERYDAY EXPERIENCE IS ALL THERE IS.

BUT ONE REBEL PRISONER ESCAPES INTO THE DAYLIGHT AND SOON FINDS THAT THERE IS A BETTER AND "MORE REAL" WORLD OUTSIDE.

Similarly, someone who has been trained in mental skills like mathematics will finally realize that there is a better and more real world of Forms beyond everyday experience. Such individuals will finally see and know "Goodness itself" and become the infallible "golden" rulers of a society made up of indoctrinated silver, bronze and iron people who never question the system. In this Republic, if anyone wanted to know what to do, they'd just ask a "Guardian".

In his later works, Plato seems to have had some doubts about the Forms and how they relate to everyday objects in the world, or "particulars". Plato's system is "closed". If you accept what he says about knowledge, then you presumably have to accept his dictatorial moral and political views. Plato seems to have thought that all knowledge can be as permanent and disembodied as mathematics – which it can't. He also probably became "bewitched" by the strange quirkiness of ancient Greek which insinuates that if you "know" anything, you have to experience it directly.

IF YOU KNOW WHAT "BEAUTY" *IS*, THEN IT IS AS IF YOU HAVE MET IT FACE TO FACE AS A *FORM*.

But it's never clear what the Forms are, where they exist, what they look like and why only a few experts ever get to "see" them.

25

PHILOSOPHICAL EXPERTS

Plato's philosophy encouraged later generations of philosophers to believe it was their job to discover special kinds of mystical or "ideal" knowledge lying below the surface of the everyday. His political philosophy is also a potentially dangerous encouragement to create a "utopia" ruled by a "superior" and authoritarian élite. We know where experiments of that kind can lead.

ARISTOTLE THE TEACHER

When he was eighteen, **Aristotle** (384-322 B.C.) came down to Athens from Macedonia in northern Greece to study in Plato's Academy. He obviously liked being a student there, because he stayed for twenty years. When Plato died, Aristotle left Athens, got married and returned home to Macedonia.

I WAS INVITED BACK BY PHILIP, RULER OF MACEDONIA, TO BECOME THE TUTOR OF HIS SON, ALEXANDER, AGED THIRTEEN.

I LATER BECAME THE CONQUEROR, ALEXANDER THE GREAT.

Eventually he returned to Athens and founded his own university called the **Lyceum**. He had to leave Athens when Alexander died, because Macedonian imperialists suddenly became extremely unpopular. He finally died in exile in Euboia in 322 B.C. In his will, he asked that his slaves be made free men, even though he had earlier suggested that such captive people were slaves "by nature".

DEDUCTIVE OR SYLLOGISTIC LOGIC

Aristotle wrote some 400 books on nearly everything – from molluscs to immortal souls.

THERE IS SOMETHING WONDERFUL ABOUT THE WHOLE OF THE NATURAL WORLD.

*PHILOSOPHERS ARE EXTREMELY GRATEFUL TO HIM BECAUSE HE INVENTED **DEDUCTIVE LOGIC** WHICH LOOKS LIKE THIS ...*

All frogs can swim (Premise)

This is a frog (Premise)

Therefore it can swim (Conclusion)

Similar logical structures or **syllogisms** can be produced with "No frogs" and "Some frogs". And if your argument follows some simple rules (like not allowing more in the conclusion than the premises), then it will be valid. And if the premises are true, and your argument is valid, then the conclusion will be guaranteed.

THE FROG **WILL** BE ABLE TO SWIM, AND YOU WON'T HAVE TO THROW IT IN THE WATER TO FIND OUT.

Logic is a powerful tool, but Aristotle was never very clear about what exactly logic is telling you about – the world itself, the human mind or how language works.

INDUCTION AND SCIENCE

Aristotle was not at all convinced by Plato's bizarre theory of Ideal Forms. He too believed that the world was made up of "forms", but these were only "natural kinds" or species. The scientist's job is to find out what all these "kinds" are, and to explore their properties. This is one reason why Aristotle also recognized the importance of **induction**. By observing particular swimming frogs we can make an informed guess that all frogs can swim.

THESE FROGS CAN SWIM ...

THEREFORE ALL FROGS CAN SWIM.

By being able to generalize from specific frogs to the species, we can start to do science. We can use inductive generalizations about the species to deduce a conclusion about an individual frog, and this gives science the power of prediction.

All frogs can swim
This is a frog
Therefore he can swim

FINAL CAUSES

Aristotle thought that only *individual* things existed, not "Forms", and that everything had a "final cause" or potential function. So fire has the constant potential to move upward and heavy objects to fall downward. Other things like plants, animals and human beings have much more complex functions.

AND BECAUSE EVERY THING AND EVENT HAS A CAUSE, IF THEY ARE ALL TRACED BACK TO THE BEGINNING OF TIME, THEN THERE MUST BE ONE FIRST CAUSE OR "PRIME MOVER" ...

This circular and rather empty account of why things behave as they do is called a **Teleological** explanation. It's as if "cause" is a mysterious internal "puller" or ultimate purpose, not an external separate "pusher". Modern philosophers and scientists are less confident about predicting what the final purpose of every-thing is. Thanks to Darwinian evo-lutionary beliefs, they even doubt whether such a thing exists.

SOMETHING VERY CLOSE TO A DIVINE CREATOR.

SOULS AND SUBSTANCES

Aristotle also had a go at the One Big Question. He didn't accept that material objects were just inferior copies of eternal "Forms". For Aristotle, everything is made of unique "substances" which have "essential" or "accidental" properties. Essential properties *define* something.

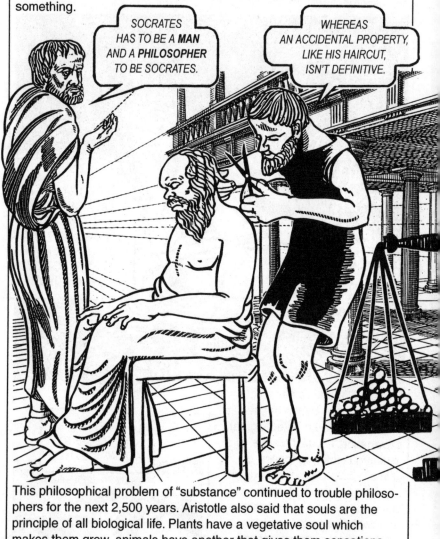

> SOCRATES HAS TO BE A **MAN** AND A **PHILOSOPHER** TO BE SOCRATES.

> WHEREAS AN ACCIDENTAL PROPERTY, LIKE HIS HAIRCUT, ISN'T DEFINITIVE.

This philosophical problem of "substance" continued to trouble philosophers for the next 2,500 years. Aristotle also said that souls are the principle of all biological life. Plants have a vegetative soul which makes them grow, animals have another that gives them sensations and humans have both, with the added bonus of reason. Unlike Pythagorean and Platonic souls though, the Aristotelian one offers no guarantee of immortality.

THE ETHICS OF MODERATION

Plato thought morality should be left to infallible experts. Aristotle thought morality was more like a practical everyday sort of skill that most adults acquire from experience. Parents train their offspring to be moral in their behaviour towards other children and adults then learn how to be sensible and moderate in their dealings with others. Human beings are social animals, programmed to live together harmoniously, even if their moral "software" needs to be exercised regularly by choosing the "Mean" between extremes.

BY ACTING MODERATELY, PEOPLE CAN BECOME "HAPPY" AS ACCOMPLISHED HUMAN BEINGS AND GOOD CITIZENS.

So Aristotelian ethics is more about self-fulfilment than morality as such.

TAKING THE BLAME

Aristotle thought Socrates was wrong to believe that "Virtue is knowledge".

*BEING A MORAL PERSON INVOLVES NOT JUST **KNOWING** WHAT IS RIGHT, BUT **CHOOSING** IT AS WELL.*

INDIVIDUALS MUST ACCEPT RESPONSIBILITY FOR THEIR VOLUNTARY ACTIONS WHICH INVOLVE OTHERS.

Aristotle's ethics may seem dull and obvious but his "virtue theory" could be right. Perhaps ethics should be about producing people who are morally experienced, rather than about inventing "pure" moral systems or rules. But do human beings have these moral "virtues" or functions? Our function might be to act as ruthless individualists.

PLATONIST DREAMERS AND ARISTOTELIAN REALISTS

Socrates, Plato and Aristotle got Western philosophy firmly established. The philosopher **A.N. Whitehead** (1861-1947) famously suggested that **all** of Western philosophy ultimately consists of no more than "footnotes" to Plato. Plato did ask all the right questions for which philosophers are still seeking answers. It is also commonly suggested that, ever since, philosophers have had either of two tendencies.

PLATONIC TENDENCIES – SEEKING HIDDEN AND ULTIMATE MYSTICAL TRUTHS THROUGH THE USE OF REASON.

OR ARISTOTELIAN ONES – BECAUSE THEY ARE METHODICAL, CAUTIOUS, AND RELY ONLY ON WHAT THEIR FIVE SENSES TELL THEM.

INTERLUDE: A BRIEF HISTORY

The independent Greek city states were eventually swallowed up by the empire of **Alexander the Great** (356-323 B.C.), Aristotle's pupil, whose conquests swept across Persia and Egypt to the borders of India. So began the **Hellenistic Age** (323-27 B.C.) when Greek culture spread throughout the Mediterranean. Alexander's generals divided up and ruled the conquered territories (a descendant of one of these was **Cleopatra** (69-30 B.C.), Queen of Egypt) until the Roman Empire took them over.

ROMANS ARE GOOD SOLDIERS, ENGINEERS AND ARCHITECTS, BUT NOT VERY INNOVATIVE PHILOSOPHERS.

THE GRAECO-EGYPTIAN CITY OF ALEXANDRIA SHELTERED MANY GREEK THINKERS LIKE EUCLID, GALEN AND PTOLEMY.

THE EPICUREANS – "CULTIVATE YOUR GARDEN"

Hellenistic philosophy fragmented into different schools influenced by Aristotle's model of the "good life", which by now no longer meant being a worthy citizen of a small city state but *survival* in a huge imperial system that was often corrupt.

Epicurus (341-270 B.C.) suggested that the individual just needed tranquillity and peace of mind to be happy. As a follower of Democritus, he maintained that death was nothing to fear – it was simply the inevitable melting of our souls and bodies into atoms.

LIFE IS SOMETHING TO BE ENJOYED BY INDULGING IN MODERATE PLEASURES AND BY CULTIVATING FRIENDSHIPS.

Personal contentment could only be achieved by retreating from the nasty and often violent world of politics, which is why Epicureans are sometimes known as the "garden" philosophers.

THE STOICS

The Stoics said that the way to lead the good life was to have faith only in reason and to distrust human emotions because, in the end, feelings always make you unhappy.

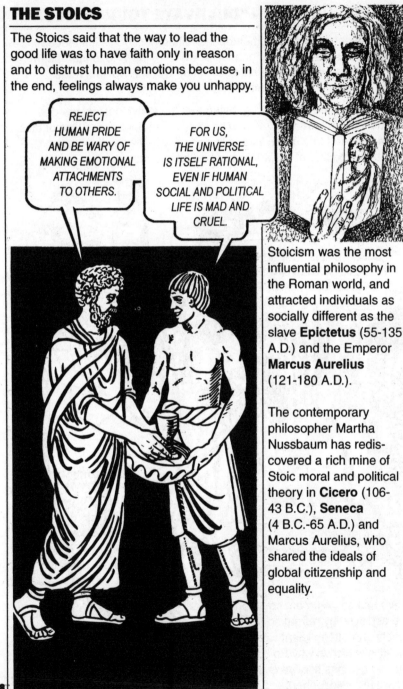

> *REJECT HUMAN PRIDE AND BE WARY OF MAKING EMOTIONAL ATTACHMENTS TO OTHERS.*

> *FOR US, THE UNIVERSE IS ITSELF RATIONAL, EVEN IF HUMAN SOCIAL AND POLITICAL LIFE IS MAD AND CRUEL.*

Stoicism was the most influential philosophy in the Roman world, and attracted individuals as socially different as the slave **Epictetus** (55-135 A.D.) and the Emperor **Marcus Aurelius** (121-180 A.D.).

The contemporary philosopher Martha Nussbaum has rediscovered a rich mine of Stoic moral and political theory in **Cicero** (106-43 B.C.), **Seneca** (4 B.C.-65 A.D.) and Marcus Aurelius, who shared the ideals of global citizenship and equality.

SCEPTICS AND CYNICS

The Sceptics also quested for the good life, but their solution was odder. Scepticism was invented by **Pyrrho** (c. 360-272 B.C.) who taught that it was unwise to believe in *anything*. He allegedly carried this belief to extremes by walking near the edges of cliffs and in front of horses, until he died at a ripe old age. **Diogenes** the Cynic (412-322 B.C.), a total anarchist, lived in a barrel and was rude to everyone, even Alexander the Great.

NO NEED TO REBEL BECAUSE EVERYONE IS ALREADY FREE.

SCEPTICISM PRODUCES HAPPINESS, BECAUSE BY HAVING NO DOGMATIC BELIEFS YOU BECOME FREE FROM WORRY.

Sextus Empiricus (c. 200 A.D.)

Like Heraclitus, Sextus pointed out that all knowledge is relative and so untrustworthy, and that nothing can ultimately ever be proved. (Any proof has itself to be proved, and what proves that proof proved, and so on, *ad infinitum*.) In the end, of course, sceptics cheat – they are always dogmatic about their one central doctrine, *relativism*.

MORE SHORT HISTORY

The Roman Empire is often said to have collapsed in the 5th century A.D., yet Rome itself remained an important Christian ecclesiastical centre thereafter. And the eastern half of the empire, or Byzantium, established in 293 A.D. with Constantinople as its capital, persisted until it fell to the Turks in 1453. Arab civilization flourished under Islam from the 7th century and spread across North Africa to Spain.

WE PRESERVED GREEK PHILOSOPHY AND SCIENCE – UNTIL THESE WERE "REDISCOVERED" BY THE WEST EMERGING FROM THE DARK AGES.

THE POST-ROMAN AGE IN EUROPE WITH ITS NOMADIC MARAUDING TRIBES AND URBAN DECAY WAS NOT A GOOD TIME FOR WESTERN PHILOSOPHY.

CHRISTIANITY ARRIVES

Constantine (c. 285-337 A.D.) was the first Roman Emperor to adopt Christianity and make it the official religion of the empire (c. 320 A.D.). So began the power of the Roman Catholic Church, which would impose its own universal culture throughout western Europe. The Church had a monopoly on all forms of philosophical thought and actively discouraged independent or unorthodox views.

READERS AND THINKERS WERE ALL CLERICS AND ECCLESIASTICAL SCHOLARS.

PHILOSOPHY BECAME THEOLOGY, PREOCCUPIED WITH RELIGIOUS QUESTIONS ABOUT THE NATURE AND EXISTENCE OF GOD.

Some philosophers like **Plotinus** (204-270 A.D.) attempted a difficult reconciliation of early Church doctrine with the works of Plato.

THE CHURCH FATHERS

The major philosophers of this period are usually known as the Church "Fathers" because they clarified and established the central doctrines and complex beliefs of the Church. They "count" as philosophers because they believed that God had endowed human beings with reason in order to argue and discuss theological problems. There was more to the Christian faith than blind superstition.

One of these "Fathers" who always insisted on the absolute authority of the Church was **St Augustine** (354-430). He was born in North Africa and wrote the famous **Confessions** about his own wicked youth.

I CONVERTED TO CHRISTIANITY AT THE AGE OF 33 AND BECAME OBSESSED BY THE PROBLEM OF EVIL IN MYSELF AND IN THE WORLD AT LARGE.

THE PROBLEM OF EVIL

He argued that evil is caused by us and not by God. The problem of evil wouldn't have arisen if God had made programmed "good" automata instead of human beings. But He generously created us as free, autonomous individuals.

UNFORTUNATELY, WE USE THIS FREEDOM TO DO WICKED THINGS AND THAT'S WHERE EVIL COMES FROM.

Augustine concluded that God always knows what moral choices we are going to make, but refrains from interfering. Augustine was also impressed by the **Teleological** argument for the existence of God. This is the doctrine of a final cause and purpose. The world is beautiful, orderly and designed, all of which points to a divine creator existing outside of time.

ST ANSELM'S PROOF

By the 11th century, philosopher-theologians were called "schoolmen" and the philosophy they produced "Scholasticism".
St Anselm (1033-1109) is famous for his extraordinary **Ontological** argument for the existence of God, which goes something like this ...

Any idea of God has to be of the greatest being that ever existed.

But the existence of something just in the mind is inferior to an existence in reality.

So, as God is the greatest conceivable being, He must exist in reality, as well as in the mind.

St Anselm seems to think that if he can frame the words correctly, then he can somehow produce a proof for God's existence. The Ontological argument is a kind of conjuring trick.

BUT IDEAS OF THINGS AND THINGS THEMSELVES ARE DIFFERENT WHERE EXISTENCE IS CONCERNED.

ABELARD'S NOMINALISM

The cleric **Peter Abelard** (1079-1144) had an affair with his student Heloise and was castrated because of it. She entered a nunnery and they spent the rest of their lives writing love letters to each other. Abelard produced some challenging ideas about the nature of language and the world.

Words in any dictionary like "cat" or "chair" are usually the names of "Universals" or classes of things. Plato thought that such words referred to special divine "Forms". Abelard maintained that there are no such entities, only individual particulars in the world. So language can often trick philosophers into believing odd things exist that don't.

AQUINAS AND NATURAL THEOLOGY

St Thomas Aquinas (1225-74) invented another argument for the existence of God, rather similar to the one produced by Aristotle about the "Prime Mover". The **Cosmological** argument points out that everything has a cause, and so eventually there must be One Big Cause of Everything – or God. Aquinas also believed in "Natural Theology".

WHEN NATURE IS OBSERVED, IT IS SEEN TO OBSERVE CERTAIN LAWS. THESE LAWS ARE ORDAINED BY GOD. SO STUDYING THE NATURAL WORLD IS ANOTHER WAY IN WHICH WE CAN UNDERSTAND THE MIND OF GOD.

This was good news for medieval scientists because it meant that science was not necessarily a heretical activity. Aquinas's doctrine also implied that on rare occasions it was acceptable to disobey secular law if you believed it came into conflict with the Law of God.

OCKHAM'S RAZOR

Later theologians like **William of Ockham** (1285-1349) pursued the Scholastic concern with knotty problems of logic, language and meaning. Ockham was another Nominalist who pointed out that a lot of academic philosophy was really no more than waffle about imaginary entities. He thought that the great truths are usually simple, so it is foolish to prefer a complicated answer to a simpler one. This principle of his is known as "Ockham's razor" and has been highly influential in science, if not philosophy itself, unfortunately.

IT IS FOOLISH TO DO WITH MORE WHAT CAN BE DONE WITH LESS.

EVERYTHING SHOULD BE MADE AS SIMPLE AS POSSIBLE, BUT NOT SIMPLER.

RENAISSANCE HUMANISM

The complex historical and cultural event known as the Renaissance began in northern Italy in the 14th century and spread throughout western Europe during the next two centuries.

RENAISSANCE "HUMANISM" MEANS THAT PHILOSOPHERS CAN NOW THINK ABOUT HUMAN ACHIEVEMENTS AND IDEAS ...

AND CONCENTRATE LESS ON THE EXISTENCE AND NATURE OF GOD.

Feudal society gradually died off. Cities became more important and the members of a modern mercantile class encouraged new ideas in mathematics, science and technology, partly because such things could make money. The other great change, the Reformation, allowed philosophers living in Protestant countries to ask more radical questions about science, politics and morality.

ERASMUS THE SCEPTIC

One philosopher who inadvertently helped to start the Protestant Reformation was **Erasmus** (1466-1536), with his book **In Praise of Folly**. Erasmus was fiercely critical of the corruption of the Catholic Church. He took no one seriously, least of all philosophers.

THEY WOULD BE THE WORST PEOPLE TO PUT IN CHARGE OF GOVERNMENT, DESPITE WHAT PLATO SAID.

Like the Sceptics before him, he also thought that human "wisdom" was illusory and unattainable.

POLITICAL THEORISTS

Aristotle had dominated most medieval theology, philosophy and science. Renaissance scientists began to discover that he was often spectacularly wrong. The Sun does not go round the Earth. Aristotle had also insisted that the aim of all political activity was to produce morally upright citizens. Two Renaissance political philosophers thought he was wrong about that as well.

Niccolò Machiavelli (1469-1527) observed the utterly unprincipled and ruthless behaviour of Italian Renaissance rulers and concluded that politics was a necessarily dirty game of treachery and deceit. In his book **The Prince** he suggested that morality and politics don't mix.

> A SUCCESSFUL RULER WILL OFTEN BE REQUIRED TO CHEAT, LIE, BREAK PROMISES, AND EVEN MURDER.

Machiavelli is more of a political theorist than a true philosopher, but his acute observation of practical politics established the principles of a modern secular **civil society**.

The Englishman **Thomas Hobbes** (1588-1679) gave a pessimistic account of human nature in his book **Leviathan**. He was fascinated by the deductive rigour of geometry and thought that logical argument could be used to produce a political philosophy. His view of human nature, sometimes called **psychological egoism**, is mechanistic and deeply cynical.

HUMAN BEINGS ARE INSTINCTIVELY SELFISH AND RUTHLESS, SO ANY ATTEMPT TO MAKE THEM MORAL BEINGS IS A WASTE OF TIME.

Left to their own devices in a "state of nature", they will inevitably kill each other. Life for everyone will soon become "solitary, poor, nasty, brutish and short".

THE SOCIAL CONTRACT THEORY

In a desperate attempt to escape from being murdered in their beds, Hobbes believed that selfish individuals would have to make a reciprocal "Social contract" with each other. But a contract between ruthless individualists would necessarily have to be reinforced by a second "Government contract" which would permit governments to punish those who broke the first.

SOVEREIGN GOVERNMENTS ARE VITAL FOR THE PRESERVATION OF HUMAN LIFE AND CIVILIZED VALUES. MORALITY IS NO MORE THAN A CYNICAL AGREEMENT BETWEEN VILLAINS.

Morality is the same as obedience to the law. It's not a very flattering account of us as a species, but at least Hobbes encouraged a new interest in human nature and a belief that governments only have the right to rule through *contract*.

BACON'S PHILOSOPHY OF SCIENCE

Francis Bacon (1561-1626) was himself a wily English politician, but as a philosopher he was more interested in the new sciences and what they could achieve. He was the first to say that "Knowledge is Power". He made no scientific discoveries himself but did take a philosophical interest in the new scientific methods of empirical observation, experimentation and induction employed by scientists like **Galileo** (1564-1642). Bacon was very dubious about Aristotle's doctrine of "final causes".

CAUSES ARE WHOLLY MATERIAL. PHYSICAL OBJECTS AND PROCESSES OBEY LAWS WHICH MEN OF COMMONSENSE WILL USUALLY DISCOVER BY USING SCIENTIFIC PROCEDURES.

His own amateur scientific investigations eventually killed him. He died of bronchitis caused by repeatedly going out in the winter weather to stuff a chicken with snow. He wanted to see if the cold would preserve it.

ORIGINS OF MODERN PHILOSOPHY

Modern philosophy is said to begin with **René Descartes** (1596-1650), the French mathematician who insisted on his own individual autonomy and refused to accept orthodox philosophical answers. He investigated the internal workings of the mind in relation to the external world and emphasized the difference between *perceiving* and *thinking*. His method of systematic doubt is introspective and autobiographical, but also determinedly objective and logical.

ALL BELIEFS MUST SUBMIT TO BEING PROVED BEYOND DOUBT. I SEEK A PHILOSOPHY THAT CAN ESTABLISH KNOWLEDGE ON A GUARANTEED BASIS.

Descartes was deeply impressed by what mathematics could achieve in sciences like astronomy. He wrote most of his philosophy in the tolerant quiet of Protestant Holland.

SCIENTIFIC DOUBT

Descartes' **Discourse on Method** (1637) seeks to discover a new kind of accurate scientific knowledge by following a few simple procedural rules. In his **Meditations** (1641), he asks if there is any kind of knowledge that can be known with certainty. By applying a technique of radically sceptical doubt, he found that he could destroy his beliefs in everything.

MY SENSES LIE TO ME. THEY INFORM ME THAT STRAIGHT STICKS IN WATER ARE BENT. THERE IS NO CONCLUSIVE WAY TO PROVE THAT ALL MY EXPERIENCES AREN'T JUST DREAMS OR HALLUCINATIONS.

Even his abstract thoughts might be illusory or wrong. An invisible demon might be hypnotizing him into thinking that he was awake and performing accurate mathematical calculations when he wasn't.

COGITO ERGO SUM

Cartesian doubt is cumulative and ruthless. Descartes suggests that there is no knowledge that can be guaranteed. He couldn't even be certain that his own body was real. But he could be certain that his *thoughts* existed. Doubting is a kind of thinking, so trying to doubt that you are thinking just doesn't work. With this insight, Descartes discovered the famous "Cogito".

> BECAUSE
> I AM THINKING, I MUST EXIST,
> AT LEAST IN SOME KIND OF MENTAL
> SENSE, OR, **COGITO ERGO SUM**.
> I THINK THEREFORE
> I AM.

From this breakthrough, Descartes went on to prove that humans are strangely dualist beings – spiritual minds or souls inhabiting material bodies. Bodies are like machines and eventually perish, but our minds are immortal. Although how the two interact is not very clear.

CLEAR AND DISTINCT IDEAS

Descartes thought that **God** would guarantee abstract rational thinking that was as "clear and distinct" as the original Cogito itself. This means that our "clear" mathematical thinking about the world is correct, but our sensory experiences of it are all subjective and flawed.

WE CAN BE CERTAIN OF THE SIZE AND WEIGHT OF AN ORANGE, BUT NOT OF ITS COLOUR, SMELL OR TASTE.

So, in the end, Descartes' scepticism is a kind of philosophical game which he uses to establish what sorts of *certain knowledge* there are.

There are numerous problems with Descartes' subjective road to a unique and personal certainty. It seems odd to believe that our senses "lie" to us. We only know that a submerged stick is straight, after all, because our eyes subsequently tell us so. It is also odd to have to rely on God as a guarantor of mathematical certainty.

DESCARTES' LEGACY

Descartes' solitary thinking **seems** to be private and inviolable, but it is still made up of words with a set of grammatical rules and a whole cultural history behind it. And perhaps any human quest for total non-human objective certainty is itself ill-conceived. Still, thanks to Descartes, later philosophers had a whole new set of questions to puzzle over ...

WHAT IS UNIQUE ABOUT HUMAN CONSCIOUSNESS?

WHAT IS THE RELATIONSHIP BETWEEN OUR MINDS AND OUR BODIES?

CAN HUMAN BEINGS EVER POSSESS CERTAINTY?

Descartes' philosophy also gave a new respectability to the dogma that true knowledge can only be derived from reason, with its accompanying assertion that empirical knowledge is second-rate, so stimulating a philosophical debate that continued for the next hundred years and more.

SPINOZA'S QUESTIONS

Baruch Spinoza (1632-77) was a Dutchman of Jewish descent who, like Descartes, also led a solitary life. As a freethinking philosopher he was excommunicated from his own Jewish community and made a meagre living as a lens-grinder, a job which eventually damaged his lungs and killed him.

Spinoza puzzled away at the problem of "substance". If, as Descartes claimed, there are two kinds of totally **self-contained** substances – the mental and the physical – how can they possibly interact?

HOW CAN A MENTAL DECISION "PUSH" SOMETHING PHYSICAL?

AND HOW CAN A PHYSICAL SENSATION AFFECT THE MIND?

Spinoza's answer in his **Ethics** (1677) was to refute Descartes' Dualism.

59

SPINOZA'S MONISM

Spinoza employed the deductive method of geometry to demonstrate that there is only *one* substance, God, in which everything else exists as a *mode*. In other words, there is one system of scientific laws from which everything in Nature can be deduced. We know only two of God's infinite attributes – **thought** (mind) and **extension** (body) – but both modes of being are the same thing differently expressed. Any object (mode of extension) is identical with a mode of thought, just as a human body has a mind. Does this mean that stones "think"?

NO, BUT IT IS A FUNDAMENTAL LAW OF NATURE THAT ALL THINGS TEND TO PERSIST IN BEING *WHAT THEY ARE.* IN THIS SENSE, "MIND" IS IN THEM.

Spinoza emphasizes the *logic* in theo*logy*, hence, for him, total scientific liberty is consistent with all that is important in the Bible. His "monism" has been wrongly confused with **pantheism** ("God is in everything") which much influenced the English and German Romantics.

LEIBNIZ AND THE MONADOLOGY

Gottfried Wilhelm Leibniz (1646-1716) was an incredibly accomplished mathematician, philosopher and statesman. In competition with **Sir Isaac Newton** (1642-1727), he laid the foundations of integral and differential calculus in his quest for "an algebra of reasoning". Critical of both Descartes and Spinoza, he proposed his own intricate metaphysical system of **Monadology** (1714).

Leibniz's central concept is that God's thinking contains an infinity of *possible worlds*, but only the *best* of them is realized. What decides the "best" is a minimum of causes (laws or means) and a maximum of effects (states or ends).

$$= \frac{x+2}{3}$$

$$\frac{1}{9} \int \quad 1 \quad -d\,x \qquad d\,u \quad = \frac{1}{3} d\,x$$

$$\frac{(x+2)^2}{9}$$

> OURS IS THE "BEST OF ALL POSSIBLE WORLDS" BECAUSE IT IS A MAXIMALLY CONSISTENT SYSTEM OF **MONADS**.

What does Leibniz mean by "monad"?

You have to imagine the monad as an **individual substance** …

1. which contains every concept consistent with it but no other
2. has no parts but the "accidents" of mental qualities and tendency
3. no causal relation between monads but only between their states
4. each monad is a microcosmic world-apart which reflects the entire macrocosm
5. this possible world exists because God created it by moral but not necessarily physical necessity.

Leibniz was known as the "Aristotle of the modern world" because he attempted the last grand theory to unify Scholastic philosophy and the new scientific rationalism. Leibniz disputed Newton's theory that space and time are absolute and infinite.

IN THE MONADIC UNIVERSE, SPACE IS RELATIVE TO THE INDIVIDUAL **PLACE** OF THINGS, AND TIME TO THEIR **SUCCESSIVE** STATES.

VOLTAIRE AND THE ENLIGHTENMENT

Leibniz produced an elaborate metaphysical model to describe the basic structure of the universe. But is it true? And how does one establish whether it is true or not? This reveals a major weakness of his and Spinoza's Rationalist philosophy. Leibniz's apparently over-optimistic view of "the best of all possible worlds" was satirized in Voltaire's novel, *Candide* (1759). **Voltaire** (1694-1778) was a great champion of the Enlightenment, an era of social radicalism and new confidence in the powers of reason over dogma, superstition and tyranny.

Along with the versatile Encyclopedist **Denis Diderot** (1713-84) and other French *philosophes*, Voltaire popularized the great English pioneers of empiricism: Bacon, Newton and Locke.

LOCKE AND BRITISH EMPIRICISM

John Locke (1632-1704) adopted many of Descartes' ideas about the mind and perception, but he was also a founder of **Empiricism**, which insists that fundamental human knowledge must come from the senses. He also thought that the Platonic and Cartesian doctrine of innate ideas was ridiculous and that most metaphysics was nonsense.

*AT BIRTH, THE HUMAN MIND IS JUST A BLANK OR "TABULA RASA" AND CAN ONLY ACQUIRE BASIC KNOWLEDGE OF THE WORLD **THROUGH THE SENSES**.*

AFTER THIS INITIAL PROCESS, EXPERIENCES CAN BE CATEGORIZED AND STORED IN THE MEMORY.

Only **then** can the mind start to assemble its own new ideas and think independently from the senses.

Locke agreed with Descartes that our experience of the world is always indirect. All that our minds actually experience are representations or mental images, which means that we cannot have any direct knowledge of the "substance" of which the world is made. Locke also agreed that our experience of any object, like an orange, is mixed.

ITS "PRIMARY" QUALITIES OF SIZE AND WEIGHT ARE "IN" THE ORANGE AND ARE OBJECTIVE AND SCIENTIFICALLY MEASURABLE.

ITS "SECONDARY" QUALITIES OF COLOUR, SMELL AND TASTE ARE JUST ITS EFFECTS ON OUR SENSE ORGANS, AND SO ARE SUBJECTIVE AND RELATIVE.

Locke's world is a monochrome and odourless place which we human beings then experience in our own uniquely colourful and smelly way. If we were from another planet and equipped with different sense organs, then oranges would still be round, but their secondary qualities might be quite changed. But Locke never doubted that there was an external world "out there" causing him to have these mental experiences.

BERKELEY'S IDEALISM

Bishop Berkeley (1685-1753) turned Locke's empiricist philosophy into something much more metaphysical – usually known as **Idealism**. He seized on the illogicalities of Locke's Primary and Secondary distinction by demonstrating that you cannot separate them. It's not possible to distinguish the primary **shape** of an object without its secondary **colour**. So why assume that some experiences are "real" and some are just "mental"? Berkeley concluded that all our experiences were mental ones caused by God and that our everyday experiences were a gigantic illusion. He formulated this in a famous maxim: *esse est percipi*, to be is to be perceived. Fortunately, God makes the illusions coherent and consistent, so that our experiences come in "bundles".

AN "ORANGE EXPERIENCE" IS A COHERENT PACKAGE OF SHAPE, COLOUR, TASTE AND SO ON.

One implication of this is that when things are not being perceived, they no longer exist. This idea is very hard to believe, but philosophers are rather fond of it, because it seems impossible to disprove. How could we "climb outside" of our senses to disprove what Berkeley says?

PERHAPS ONE DAY WE WILL BE ABLE TO ASK THOSE INHABITANTS FROM ANOTHER PLANET WITH DIFFERENT SENSE ORGANS **AND** A DIFFERENT RELIGION.

The doctrine of "Idealism" (only "ideas" exist) is, however, vulnerable to Ockham's razor – to assume that it is indeed the external world that causes our experiences, rather than an exceedingly busy deity, would be a simpler explanation.

HUME AND EMPIRICAL SCEPTICISM

David Hume (1711-76), a chief figure of the Scottish Enlightenment who knew the leading French *philosophes*, was an atheist and scathing about traditional theological arguments which claimed to "prove" the existence of God. As a committed empiricist, he was also extremely sceptical about the assertions made by Rationalists about the powers and extent of human reason. Like Berkeley, he is a bit of a philosopher's philosopher, because many of his ideas are rather technical but important to modern philosophy.

Hume recognized the major weakness of **Induction** as a source of knowledge, against empiricists like Bacon, who thought that Induction was a reliable foundation for all science.

*IF ALL THE SWANS YOU HAVE PERSONALLY OBSERVED HAVE BEEN WHITE, THEN IT IS SCIENTIFICALLY VERY PROBABLE THAT SO ARE ALL THE SWANS IN THE WORLD – UNTIL YOU VISIT AUSTRALIA AND SEE A **BLACK** ONE. THEN WHAT HAPPENS?*

Hume is only pointing out that all scientific findings based on observation and induction must remain conjectural and temporary. Induction can never offer you the certainty that logic can.

THE PROBLEM OF CAUSATION

Hume was the first philosopher to clarify what causation is. Medieval philosophers like St Thomas Aquinas had a firm belief in the **certainty** of causation – it proved God's existence. Hume analyzed the concept of "cause" and found that it was really no more than a human belief based on past experiences. Everyone likes to think that all events have causes.

> WE BELIEVE THAT THERE IS ALWAYS A CAUSE FOR MACHINES BREAKING DOWN, FOR PLANTS GROWING AND FOR PLANETS CIRCLING THE SUN. THESE ARE ALL PERFECTLY SANE BELIEFS, BUT ONLY BELIEFS NEVERTHELESS.

They are all based on induction – our observation of machines, plants and planets in the past – but none of them has any logical certainty.

Hume also recognized that it is not possible to **prove** moral beliefs. The concept of "wicked-ness" is not something you can see. You can prove facts like "Socrates is mortal", provided you know that all men are mortal and Socrates is a man.

MORAL SCEPTICISM

BUT YOU CAN'T LOGICALLY PROVE THAT "STEALING IS WRONG" FROM FACTS, BECAUSE THIS CONCLUSION IS FINALLY ONLY A BELIEF OR OPINION.

IN DEDUCTIVE LOGIC, YOU CAN'T HAVE A VALID **BELIEF-CONCLUSION** THAT EMERGES FROM SOME **FACT-PREMISES**.

Hume's view of moral philosophy is sometimes called "Subjectivism". This is the belief that moral propositions such as "Hitler was evil" refer only to the subjective feelings of one individual ("I dislike Hitler"). Hume thought that there were virtually no human beliefs that could be "proved", and that "reason" was greatly overrated. Although he was a radical philosopher, he had conservative personal beliefs which led him to suggest that human beings could only ever be content if they relied on their natural feelings of sympathy for each other and respected all social traditions.

Rather disturbingly, Hume also had doubts about the existence of the Self, because of its undetectability: "Whenever I ask what I call myself … I always stumble on some perception or other … but I can never catch myself at any time, without a perception."

ROUSSEAU'S PRIMITIVE STATE OF INNOCENCE

Voltaire greatly admired John Locke's political writings on "Natural Rights". Locke maintained that individuals have certain inalienable rights to property, freedom of speech and worship, and even the right to rebel against unjust governments and laws. But it was the Swiss pre-Romantic, **Jean-Jacques Rousseau** (1712-78) who became the most influential political thinker of the late 18th century. Rousseau rejected the Hobbesian doctrine of an innately wicked human nature.

THE LIVES OF PRE-CIVILIZED "NATURAL" HUMAN BEINGS WERE ONES OF CONTENTMENT AND BENEVOLENCE. BUT WHEN THE GREAT HUMAN INVENTIONS OF CIVILIZATION AND PRIVATE PROPERTY ARRIVED, EVERYTHING WENT DOWNHILL.

Artificial needs stimulated artificial greeds. This is why, in his view, pre-societal beings like children and savages are morally superior. It's a "back to nature" myth that influenced the cultural movement known as Romanticism.

THE GENERAL WILL

More ominously, Rousseau believed that society's laws should be an expression of "The General Will" which would always be right. It is not clear how this could be established and when it would have to be enforced. Unfortunately, revolutionary situations always throw up ruthless idealists and opportunists, ready to declare themselves the personal embodiments of this abstract entity, who then impose it violently on others.

THIS IS ONE REASON WHY THE IDEALISM OF THE 1789 FRENCH REVOLUTION SOON TURNED INTO "THE TERROR" OF 1792.

KANT'S RESPONSE TO HUME

Immanuel Kant (1724-1804) was a meticulous bachelor of such regular habits that the citizens of Königsberg could set their watches by his daily routine walks. His faithful servant Lampe always followed him with an umbrella, "just in case". Kant said he was awoken from his Rationalist "dogmatic slumbers" by reading Hume. But he disagreed with Hume's assertion that we believe in causation because we are indoctrinated by our past experiences of the world.

MY RESPONSE WAS TO ARGUE AGAINST HUME THAT OUR KNOWLEDGE OF THE WORLD CANNOT COME FROM OBSERVATION ALONE.

THEY SAY HERR PROFESSOR KANT LIKES THE COMPANY OF BEAUTIFUL AND INTELLIGENT WOMEN.

YES, AND HIS STUDENTS ENJOY HIS LECTURES, WHICH ARE SAID TO BE VERY DIFFICULT.

Kant proposed that human beings "see" causation in the world because they are *constituted* that way. He was the first philosopher to show that neither Rationalists nor Empiricists had got it quite right.

73

MENTAL STRUCTURES PRECEDE EXPERIENCE

In his **Critique of Pure Reason** (1781), Kant shows how the attempts to use reason to establish metaphysical "truths" always produce impossible contradictions. He then demonstrates how we acquire knowledge of the world. The human mind is active, not a passive recipient of information. When we look at the world we "constitute" it in order to make sense of it. Some of the concepts that we apply to our present experiences do indeed come from our past ones, but the most important ones **precede** experience. They are **a priori** – prior to our experiences.

THE MIND ORGANIZES AND SYSTEMATIZES WHAT WE EXPERIENCE WITH ITS OWN PROGRAMMED "INTUITIONS" AND "CATEGORIES" WHICH MAKE SENSE OF ALL THE DATA THAT CONSTANTLY FLOODS IN THROUGH OUR SENSES.

Hume claimed that we gradually build up our conceptual apparatus from our experiences. Kant replies that unless we have some kind of mental conceptual apparatus to begin with, no experiences would ever be possible. So he is a kind of sophisticated **idealist**. "*Thoughts without content are empty, intuitions without concepts are blind.*"

PHENOMENAL AND NOUMENAL WORLDS

Even more fundamentally, our every experience must also be encountered through the "forms of intuition" of time and space. So, to some extent, our experience of the world is our very own creation, organized by us. There are, however, strict limits on *what* we experience and *how* we experience it. We cannot choose the "input" that our sense organs give us, and we cannot alter the way our minds are devised.

ALL WE CAN EVER EXPERIENCE IS THE "PHENOMENAL" WORLD, WHICH MAY NOT BE AT ALL LIKE THE REAL "NOUMENAL" ONE. ONLY GOD CAN SEE THAT, AS HE IS UNRESTRICTED BY TIME AND SPACE AND THE LIMITATIONS OF THE HUMAN MIND.

Kant concluded that human science deals with the phenomenal world (things as they "appear"), and religion remains in the unknowable noumenal one (things as they really "are"), so science and religion need not conflict with each other. But if all we can ever experience is the phenomenal world, how can he be so confident about the existence of a noumenal one?

CATEGORICAL IMPERATIVES

Kant claimed that, unlike material objects, we can escape the phenomenal world of causation. We must have free-will if we are to choose to be moral beings. "*Ought implies Can.*"

If we are to be virtuous, we must do our duty and ignore our inclinations. Being a moral person means **not** doing what comes naturally and usually involves an internal struggle against our wicked desires. By using reason we can then discover what our duty is – obeying a set of compulsory rules or **categorical imperatives**. Kant suggests that "*one should only act on a principle that one can will to be universal law*".

IT WORKS LIKE THIS: IF WE DECIDE TO LIE, WE IMAGINE WHAT WOULD HAPPEN IF EVERYBODY LIED.

LYING ITSELF WOULD BECOME NORMAL. THE CONCEPT OF TRUTH (AND LYING ITSELF!) WOULD DISAPPEAR. LANGUAGE, LOGIC, MEANING AND ALL HUMAN COMMUNICATION WOULD DISAPPEAR INTO A NIGHTMARISH ILLOGICAL VACUUM.

So, lying is irrational and therefore wrong. Kant believed in God and thought that religion enabled ordinary people to make sense of a world that often seems immoral. But perhaps there is more to morality than always obeying a set of compulsory moral rules, regardless of individual circumstances. We can think of occasions when lying might actually be the moral thing to do.

HEGEL'S DIALECTIC

Georg Wilhelm Friedrich Hegel (1770-1831) believed, rather overconfidently, that his own unique systematic philosophy would reveal the final truths about the *whole* of reality and *all* of human history. Hegelian philosophy is breathtakingly comprehensive and written in abstract Hegelian jargon which makes it difficult to understand.

Until Hegel came on the scene, philosophers thought that Aristotle had discovered logic and that was that.

BUT THERE IS ANOTHER LOGIC. KNOWLEDGE HAS AN EVOLUTIONARY HISTORY THAT IS MADE UP OF CONCEPTS, NOT ISOLATED TRUE OR FALSE FACTUAL PROPOSITIONS.

Ideas grow and gradually move towards a better grasp of reality in a process he called the **Dialectic**.

DIALECTICAL LOGIC

History is always about a struggle between different dynamic concepts which claim to be an accurate description of reality. But any concept or **thesis** will automatically give birth to its opposite or **antithesis** and a struggle between them will occur, until a higher, more truthful **synthesis** is eventually achieved.

THIS NEW CONCEPT WILL IN TURN GENERATE ITS OWN ANTITHESIS, AND SO THE PROCESS WILL INEXORABLY CONTINUE UNTIL FINALLY "THE ABSOLUTE IDEA" IS REACHED.

This is an evolutionary and religious account of the human mind and civilization, both of which go through many stages until "absolute consciousness" and social harmony are achieved. The study of history, thought Hegel, would eventually reveal something rather like the mind of God.

THESIS ANTITHESIS SYNTHESIS

HUMAN CONSCIOUSNESS AND KNOWLEDGE

Hegelian metaphysics is about the very nature of thought itself. Hegel thought that philosophy had become too narrowly focused on isolated technical questions about knowledge and needed to look more carefully at the historical processes of human thought and culture that produce it. He was an "Idealist" like Kant, so agreed with him that we never experience the world directly through the senses, but always in a way that involves mediation or filtering by our consciousness. Hegel went even further.

ANTITHESIS ANTITHESIS SYNTHESIS THE ABSOLUTE IDEA SYNTHESIS

REALITY IS CONSTITUTED BY THE MIND AND IS ITS CREATION. THERE IS NO "NOUMENAL" WORLD.

Human consciousness itself is never fixed but continually changing and developing new categories and concepts. These determine how we experience the world, so that knowledge is always contextually dependent and always the result of a series of conflicting positions.

RELATIVE AND ABSOLUTE KNOWLEDGE

Any philosophical account of what is "objective" as opposed to "subjective" is wholly misleading. Philosophers will never be able to produce something like "complete philosophical truth" because ideas by their very nature are always changing. Knowledge is a dynamic cultural and historical process, not some timeless product waiting to be discovered "out there". This makes Hegel sound like a prophet of postmodernism when he stresses that there can be no objective stable facts or truths in a constantly changing dialectic. But he did believe that this always-shifting dialectical process must culminate in a final stage in which human beings would reach the "actual knowledge of what is".

Hegel also had a new and profound way of thinking about individual consciousness and personal freedom.

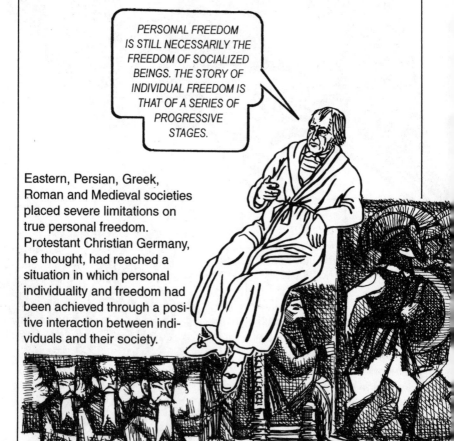

PERSONAL FREEDOM IS STILL NECESSARILY THE FREEDOM OF SOCIALIZED BEINGS. THE STORY OF INDIVIDUAL FREEDOM IS THAT OF A SERIES OF PROGRESSIVE STAGES.

Eastern, Persian, Greek, Roman and Medieval societies placed severe limitations on true personal freedom. Protestant Christian Germany, he thought, had reached a situation in which personal individuality and freedom had been achieved through a positive interaction between individuals and their society.

THE STATE AND
THE END OF HISTORY

Hegel looked to his own autocratic Prussian state as some kind of "super-person" which had reached the final evolutionary stage. He and his fellow citizens were merely a small part of this larger organic entity and got their identity and moral status from it.

THE ACTUAL
IS THE RATIONAL.

Hegel sincerely believed that he had completed Kant's work by producing a standpoint of absolute knowledge from which the "end of history" could be predicted. His determinist dialectical process would end when the one "Spirit" guiding all reality and human reason was finally revealed. The process of getting there would be hard going because it involved incessant conflict between huge and often ruthless historical forces. Undeniably, there has been plenty of that in Europe since 1807, when the **Phenomenology of Spirit** was first published. It now seems rather doubtful that human history has a predictable "destiny" or ultimate purpose of the Hegelian or any kind.

SCHOPENHAUER'S CONCEPT OF WILL

One German philosopher hostile to Hegelian methods and doctrines was **Arthur Schopenhauer** (1788-1860). He thought that Hegel's belief in a happy ending to human history was the ramblings of a "stupid and clumsy charlatan". Another convinced Idealist, he also agreed with Kant that human beings can only ever live in the phenomenal world. But for Schopenhauer, the phenomenal world is an illusory one, always controlled by the **Will**. The Will directs every living being, including humans.

IT IS WHOLLY PURPOSELESS, A KIND OF IMPETUS WHICH FORCES ALL LIVING THINGS TO MATE, BREED AND DIE.

Human beings like to believe that their own individual lives have some kind of higher meaning, but there is no more to their lives than the urge to satisfy new desires. Different individual wills then inevitably come into conflict, and this is what produces human suffering.

THE ONLY WAY TO ESCAPE THIS TREADMILL IS TO PUT AN END TO DESIRE.

One way of doing this is to engage in artistic activities or contemplation, another is to lead a life of ascetic self-denial. Schopenhauer was the first great Western philosopher to be influenced by Buddhism. His ideas, neglected today, had a great impact on such figures as the composer **Richard Wagner** (1813-83) and the German philosopher **Nietzsche**.

NIETZSCHE: THE ANTI-CHRIST

Friedrich Nietzsche (1844-1900), although raised as a strict Lutheran like so many other German philosophers, became hostile to Christianity and totally rejected beliefs in any kind of "transcendent" or "noumenal" world.

GOD IS DEAD ... AND WE HAVE KILLED HIM.

His training as a classical philologist made him see the world of the ancient Greeks as superior to the modern Christian world with its enthusiasms for passive suffering, guilt and eternal damnation. His energetic and creative ancient Greeks wisely accepted fate and celebrated the fact that human suffering could produce lives that were both tragic and noble.

BEYOND GOOD AND EVIL

Like most philosophers before him, Nietzsche attempted to redefine human nature. He thought that it was wrong to generalize about individual human beings because it reduced them to a falsifying "common nature". He prophesied that modern capitalism and technological progress would merely produce a bourgeois world of mediocre "last men".

I WANT HUMAN BEINGS TO BECOME SOMETHING MORE – SUPERMEN OR ÜBERMENSCH.

Judaeo-Christian culture favoured the weak and commonplace, whereas the *Übermensch* would need to reject "the morality of the herd" and look "beyond" traditional notions of good and evil to something more radical and individually creative, the "Will to Power". Although Nietzsche's views about the *Übermensch* have nothing whatsoever to do with class or racial characteristics, they are certainly gender-specific – he was undoubtedly sexist. His philosophy of the "Will to Power" was later hijacked to promote a Nazi anti-Semitic doctrine.

POSTMODERN FORECAST

Nietzsche's radical scepticism does not accept that there can be any moral facts or universal moral rules based on "reason" – only contemporary prejudices that suit people's needs. All conceptual knowledge is based on generalizations determined by the ideologies and classification systems of the time, which inevitably blank out individuality and uniqueness. Most claims to eternal "truths" are no more than temporarily useful beliefs that change as history moves on.

> TRUTH, LIKE MORALITY, IS A RELATIVE MATTER. THERE ARE NO FACTS, ONLY INTERPRETATIONS.

Nietzsche forecasts postmodernism. He prefigures Wittgenstein and Derrida in first "deconstructing" beliefs as language traps. ("We shall never be rid of God until we are rid of grammar.") Foucault's histories of knowledge owe enormously to Nietzsche's ideas of genealogies and Will to Power.

ETERNAL RECURRENCE

Nietzsche also proposed a "joyous science" of **eternal recurrence**, an idea suggested by the pre-Socratic thinker Heraclitus, which argues that time is cyclical, repeating itself time and again. This was Nietzsche's sly criticism of Kant's moral imperative and Schopenhauer's gloomy view of desire as the cause of suffering. Eternal recurrence is the criterion by which to judge the value of one's life.

IF YOU'RE REALLY LIVING A GOOD LIFE, WOULDN'T YOU BE HAPPY TO REPEAT IT AGAIN AND AGAIN?

In this way, life is not judged by its "end", as in Christianity, but positively as a choice now, at this moment. Nietzsche's idea of present choice that confirms the value of existence makes him a precursor of Existentialism.

KIERKEGAARD'S CHRISTIAN EXISTENTIALISM

The Danish philosopher **Søren Kierkegaard** (1813-55) disagreed with Kant's view that religious belief and morality could be founded on reason. Faith was utterly irrational and completely unproveable. He also objected to Hegelian "both/and" dialectical processes which seemed to swallow people up and ignored the reality of their need to make individual "either/or" decisions.

Kierkegaard's main concern was with the problem of existence. Hence, his philosophy is known as a precursor of Existentialism. Most people usually ignore questions about the meaning of their lives and prefer to escape into some kind of anonymous routine. For Kierkegaard, that wasn't good enough.

EXISTENCE MEANS YOU HAVE THE FREEDOM TO CHOOSE WHO YOU ARE, AND THIS MEANS LIVING A LIFE OF COMMITMENT.

All human beings are condemned to live lives of uncertainty and absurdity, committed to subjective truths that can never be proved.

THE LEAP OF FAITH

For Kierkegaard, this meant becoming a committed Christian by making a "leap of faith", because the central beliefs of Christianity are also essentially unknowable. He concluded that you can choose to lead the *moral* life, the *aesthetic* life or the *religious* life. Kierkegaard went for the last option.

I REALIZE THAT THIS MEANS LIVING A LIFE OF "FEAR AND TREMBLING" IN MY OWN PERSONAL COVENANT WITH GOD.

One becomes Christian in the face of an "objective uncertainty" that God has no proof. This is not the "public Christendom" which Kierkegaard fiercely criticized in his own Lutheran society. His faith is ironic, playful and passionate, and he wrote like a novelist, using many pseudonyms, in combat against dry abstract philosophizing.

FROM IDEALISM TO MATERIALISM

For over eighty years, German Idealist philosophy maintained that the world was constituted by ideas, even if there was disagreement about the nature of these ideas and human knowledge of them. **Ludwig Feuerbach** (1804-72) was a key figure of change in giving a new twist to Hegel's concept of **alienation**. According to Hegel, consciousness progresses by posing contradictory difference within itself and then attempting by further insight to overcome this contradiction or self-alienation. So, if that's the way mind progresses, then, in Feuerbach's view, the error of religion becomes obvious.

*WE PROJECT ALL OUR OWN **UNREALIZED** PERFECTION ONTO AN IMAGINARY NON-HUMAN ENTITY, GOD, INSTEAD OF CONCERNING OURSELVES WITH THE REALIZABLE IMPROVEMENT OF OUR FELLOW HUMAN BEINGS.*

Later, he moved from a "Left Hegelian" criticism of religious illusion to radical **materialism**: "You are what you eat", he said, meaning that material wants come first, ideas are secondary. Feuerbach's marriage of Hegelianism and materialism opened the way for Karl Marx.

MARX'S DIALECTICAL MATERIALISM

Karl Marx (1818-83) started out as a young "Left Hegelian" but developed a new dialectical materialist model of history. His philosophy is an original mixture of German Idealism, English political economy and French socialism.

MY DIALECTICAL METHOD IS NOT ONLY DISTINCT FROM THE HEGELIAN METHOD BUT IS ABSOLUTELY OPPOSED TO IT.

PHILOSOPHERS HAVE ONLY INTERPRETED THE WORLD IN VARIOUS WAYS; THE POINT IS TO CHANGE IT.

Hegel's dialectics made human history into a progressive story of increasing human freedoms, culminating in the absolute liberty of the Prussian state. For Marx, this was Hegel "standing on his head"; in other words, "consciousness does not determine life, but life determines consciousness". Thought does not and cannot create reality; but economic realities *can* determine how people think.

For Marx, history is the story of a constant dialectical struggle, not between abstract Hegelian ideas but between all too real classes and economic forces. This is why his philosophy is sometimes called **Dialectical Materialism**. These historical struggles were originally between slaves and their owners, and then between serfs and their feudal masters. In modern society, the economic civil war is now between the bourgeoisie – the owners of capital and the means of production – and the proletariat, the industrial urban workers who sell their labour. This dialectical warfare must unavoidably end in an international workers' revolution, transforming all human society and history.

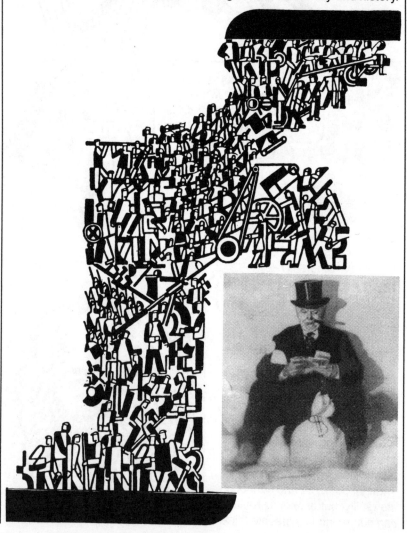

A PHILOSOPHY OF ECONOMICS

Marx was an economic determinist who claimed that all human beliefs and activities, including religion and philosophy, have always ultimately been produced by material forces. The economic **base** of any system of economic relations and productive forces will determine and drive the **superstructure** of its legal, political and cultural institutions. The primary role of these institutions is to secrete and disseminate **ideology**, so that "The ruling ideas of each age [are] the ideas of the ruling class". This means that virtually everyone, both capitalists and their victims, suffer from "false consciousness" – an inability to recognize that the exploitation of one class by another is taking place.

SURPLUS VALUE

The labour theory of value proposed by the economist **David Ricardo** (1772-1823) said that commodities get their value from the hours of work put into them. Marx went further. For him, this means that the owners of capital exploit their workforce by stealing the extra hours of work or **surplus value** of everything that they produce.

A WORKER WILL SOON PRODUCE ENOUGH GOODS TO PAY FOR HIS WAGES, THE MACHINERY HE USES AND THE BUILDING HE WORKS IN.

BUT HE WORKS MORE HOURS THAN HIS NECESSITIES REQUIRE. SO, THE CAPITALIST EMPLOYER GETS THE REST.

Workers are the real wealth producers, but they are **alienated** from what they produce – they do not see that it really belongs to them. "*The labour of the many transforms itself into the capital of the privileged few.*"

THE END OF CAPITALISM

Thanks to another economist, **Adam Smith** (1723-90), most 19th century Europeans thought that capitalism was inevitable or even God-given. Marx thought that his scientific approach to economics could accurately predict the final implosion of the capitalist system. Wealth would become concentrated in the hands of the few, whilst the vast majority of the population would be driven into poverty.

THERE WILL BE A CRISIS OF OVERPRODUCTION, AND CAPITALISM MUST COLLAPSE.

There would then be a revolution, and a Communist society would arise in which everyone would give according to their ability and take according to their needs.

THE PROPHET MARX

Marx always claimed that he was not a "Marxist". Although he took himself and his ideas very seriously, he was not always happy about being regarded by some of his disciples as an infallible prophet. Nowadays, economists are less convinced that their discipline can be made into a "science" with such correspondingly reliable predictive accuracy. Many of Marx's predictions now seem to be wrong.

> CAPITALISM APPEARS TO BE REMARKABLY RESILIENT.

> AND MOST MODERN COMMUNIST SOCIETIES, OSTENSIBLY FOUNDED ON MARXIST PRINCIPLES, HAVE BEEN ECONOMICALLY AND MORALLY DISASTROUS.

Marx's philosophy isn't very clear about exactly how a society's economic base causes its political and cultural superstructure. Some Marxists like **Herbert Marcuse** (1898-1979) of the "Frankfurt School" eventually came to believe that the "superstructure" actually has a life of its own.

96

Ideas may be as important as economics in determining human thought and history, which means that Hegel may have got something right after all. Other "post-Marxist" philosophers and activists who agree include **Antonio Gramsci** (1891-1937) who suggested that people come to regard the ideological constructs of their social and political world as "natural".

WHICH MEANS THAT GOVERNMENTS FIND IT RELATIVELY EASY TO PERSUADE PEOPLE TO ACQUIESCE IN THEIR OWN OPPRESSION.

THE DOMINANT DISCOURSE CONSISTS OF AN ELABORATE SYSTEM OF SIGNS THAT TOGETHER CONSTITUTE POWERFUL AND CONVINCING MYTHS, AND IT IS THOSE THAT FORM SOCIAL AND CULTURAL "REALITY".

Roland Barthes (1915-80), the Post-Structuralist, subsequently showed how this "naturalization" process works.

UTILITARIANISM: THE MORAL SCIENCE

At the same time that Marx was scribbling away in the British Museum Library, a very different kind of atheistic and materialist philosophy had taken root in England, called **Utilitarianism**. It was founded by **Jeremy Bentham** (1748-1832) and later refined by **John Stuart Mill** (1806-73). Unlike Marx, both Englishmen thought that there was nothing intrinsically wrong with capitalism – it was inevitable and good.

Bentham was an eccentric lawyer interested in the relationship between morality and the law.

THE ENGLISH LEGAL SYSTEM WAS FOUNDED ON AN UNSCIENTIFIC JUMBLE OF HISTORICAL PREJUDICE AND RELIGIOUS SUPERSTITION. IT IS *NONSENSE ON STILTS*.

So he put forward his own new ethical and political system based on a "scientific" definition of human nature.

All human beings are pain-pleasure organisms. Moral and political philosophy should therefore seek to increase pleasure and minimize pain. It should be democratic.

SO THE JOB OF ANY ELECTED GOVERNMENT IS TO ENSURE THE GREATEST HAPPINESS OF THE GREATEST NUMBER.

Bentham genuinely believed that "happiness" could be quantified and scientifically measured, so that moral and political issues could be "solved". This he called a "felicific (happiness-making) calculus". He also thought that the capitalist system was the best adapted to producing large amounts of material happiness.

PUBLIC HAPPINESS

As a way of organizing the priorities of a populist, democratic government, Utilitarianism obviously makes sense. Give the people what they want, or anyway, what the government thinks is good for them. It encouraged Victorian ideals of public utility, like laying drains and building schools and hospitals, because such things produced happiness. Bentham also thought that governments should penalize the work-shy with poorhouses and the criminal classes with "panopticon" prisons in which each prisoner is perpetually watched from a central tower.

THE TYRANNY OF THE MAJORITY AND PLURALISM

John Stuart Mill tried to modify Bentham's original doctrine. He worried that Utilitarianism would automatically lead to a "tyranny of the majority". If the majority believe that they will only be happy when harsh measures are inflicted on minority groups like gypsies and New Age travellers, then that's what the government is obliged to do. Utilitarianism makes no convincing provision for individual human rights. And, because there has to be some kind of central agency distributing amounts of happiness, central governments and their bureaucratic agencies become exceedingly powerful.

This troubled Mill. In **On Liberty** (1859), he advocated a tolerance for minority ideas and lifestyles, provided they do not harm others.

A PLURALIST SOCIETY IS A HEALTHY ONE, PARTLY BECAUSE IT PROVIDES AN ARENA IN WHICH "TRUTH" WILL ULTIMATELY TRIUMPH OVER FALSEHOOD. THERE'S MORE TO MORALITY THAN MAJORITY RULE.

Mill also seemed to recognize that the foundations of Bentham's Utilitarianism are themselves rather dodgy. Even if individuals are biologically programmed to seek their own happiness, what incentives does Utilitarianism offer them to procure the happiness of others?

ORIGINS OF AMERICAN PHILOSOPHY

America is a European invention, partly because its constitution is based on the philosophical principles of the Enlightenment. After the War of Independence (1774-81), the so-called "founding fathers" had to decide what America's political future would be. There was much debate about the role of central government and the extent of its powers. A surprisingly large number of American politicians were actually suspicious of democratic institutions. But others like **Thomas Jefferson** (1743-1826) and **Benjamin Franklin** (1706-90) took their new European political and philosophical ideas very seriously, and eventually their views triumphed. America became a democratic republic.

LOCKE MAINTAINED THAT THE AUTHORITY OF GOVERNMENTS SHOULD ALWAYS BE REGARDED AS PROVISIONAL.

GOVERNMENTS HAVE A CONTRACTUAL OBLIGATION TOWARDS THOSE WHO VOTE FOR THEM.

SO, OSTENSIBLY, THE GOVERNMENT ONLY EXISTS IN ORDER TO GUARANTEE ITS CITIZENS RIGHTS LIKE THOSE OF LIFE, LIBERTY AND THE PURSUIT OF HAPPINESS.

NO GOVERNMENT IS THE BEST GOVERNMENT

One early American philosopher who thought that liberty and happiness were best achieved without the help of governments was **Henry David Thoreau** (1817-62). Thoreau abandoned society for two years, two months and two days. He decided to live in a rustic hut by a Massachusetts pond where he wrote **Walden** (1854), which celebrated the quiet beauties of his natural surroundings and recommended the simple life.

OUR LIFE IS FRITTERED AWAY BY DETAIL ... SIMPLICITY, SIMPLICITY.

One day in 1846, Thoreau left his cabin and sauntered into town to get a shoe mended. Unfortunately, the town constable saw him and demanded he pay his poll tax. Thoreau believed that his taxes would be used to support the war against Mexico and bolster the slavery laws, so he refused to pay and went to jail for a night. He wrote his deeply Romantic and anarchistic **Civil Disobedience** as a result.

MY ESSAY RECOMMENDS "PASSIVE RESISTANCE" AS A MEANS OF PROTEST AGAINST WICKED GOVERNMENTS.

Bob Dylan

Noam Chomsky

Allen Ginsberg

Mahatma Gandhi (1869-1948)

I USED "PASSIVE RESISTANCE" TO CONFRONT AND FINALLY DEFEAT THE BRITISH EMPIRE IN INDIA.

The noble tradition of disrespect continues to this day. Many good Americans like **Noam Chomsky** (b. 1928) still believe in the priority of the individual conscience over state authority and wisely remain suspicious of large corporations and government agencies that now largely define their country and its foreign policy. Beatnik and Hippie "alternatives" can be traced back to Thoreau's anarchistic dissidence.

EMERSON: THE KNOWLEDGE THAT LIES BEYOND

Thoreau didn't develop his ideas about the individual conscience in splendid rural isolation. He was part of a uniquely American literary and philosophical movement known as **Transcendentalism**. When philosophy is labelled as "transcendent" it is usually because it makes metaphysical claims for a higher and truer knowledge which is somehow beyond ordinary human sense-experience and so reachable only through reason or intuition. Plato's "Forms" and medieval theological speculations about the nature of God would be good examples. For Kant, such transcendent knowledge was unreachable, although it was possible to deduce some transcendental knowledge of the categories and intuitions that make all human experience possible.

The Transcendentalism of **Ralph Waldo Emerson** (1803-82) is a unique and rather odd mixture of Platonism, Kant, Hinduism, German Idealism and English Romanticism. It is profoundly mystical and emphasizes the priority of **intuition** and individual conscience over state authority and organized religion.

NOTHING IS AT LAST SACRED BUT THE INTEGRITY OF YOUR OWN MIND.

Transcendentalists like Emerson and Thoreau held pantheistic views about the beauty of the natural world, a beauty which existed because of the divinity residing in all earthly things (a philosophical view which is actually rather untranscendent). Emerson suggested that the fundamental purpose of human life is an ultimate union with the "over-soul" – an amorphous entity somewhat akin to Spinoza's monist substance or Hegel's "Spirit". Transcendentalism is an odd derivative amalgam of many different European (and Eastern) philosophical and literary traditions which really makes it an interesting social and literary phenomenon, rather than a philosophical one.

BOTH THOREAU AND I WERE CRITICAL OF AN AMERICA THAT WE SAW BECOMING INCREASINGLY MATERIALIST, URBAN AND INDUSTRIAL.

In his later years, Emerson became active in the abolitionist cause and gave many anti-slavery speeches throughout the Northern States. The benign influence of both men on American cultural and political life is immense. "*Whoso would be a man must be a non-conformist.*"

PRAGMATISM

But the most important and truly independent American philosophy is **Pragmatism**. **Charles Sanders Peirce** (1839-1914) and **William James** (1842-1910) were both radical empiricists, so somewhat hostile to the sorts of metaphysical speculation permitted by Transcendentalism. Pragmatism rejected the traditional rationalist and empiricist philosophical views of knowledge as some kind of private mental experience. It suggested that human knowledge should be envisaged more as an adaptive response to the environment in its ability to solve problems.

AN IDEA MAY BE STRINGENTLY ARGUED, BUT IF IT DOESN'T MAKE ANY DIFFERENCE TO EVERYDAY LIFE, THEN IT ISN'T IMPORTANT OR "TRUE".

HUMAN THEORIES MAKE SENSE ONLY IF THEY HAVE "CASH VALUE" BY BEING USEFUL.

SO, IN THE END, EVEN TRANSCENDENTALIST MYSTICISM IS "USEFUL" IF IT HELPED SOME 19TH CENTURY AMERICANS MAKE SENSE OF THEIR LIVES.

C.S. PEIRCE

The most profound and original pragmatist is undoubtedly C.S. Peirce. He is only recently being credited with single-handedly preparing the ground for much 20th century philosophy. Like Thoreau, he never really "fitted" into respectable American society. He published no books in his own lifetime, lived much of his life as a recluse and died in poverty. In his early years he was a practising physicist and made some important discoveries in geophysics. He also made some major contributions towards formal logic and the philosophy of science. His own radical empiricist philosophy anticipates the views of the Logical Positivists, as we'll see.

THERE ARE NO "ULTIMATE TRUTHS" THAT PHILOSOPHY CAN ESTABLISH ABOUT THE NATURE OF "REALITY". INDIVIDUAL IDEAS MUST ALWAYS BE TESTED BY THE EFFECTS THEY PRODUCE.

He called himself a "contrite fallibilist" because he recognized that all human scientific knowledge is always provisional, so he anticipated the "Falsificationism" of **Karl Popper** (see page 150).

SEMIOTICS

More importantly, he more or less invented **Semiotics** – the theory of Signs – a discipline crucial to the development of 20th century Structuralism and Postmodernism. Peirce classified signs as *natural* (clouds signify rain, spots signify measles), *iconic* (where the sign resembles that which is signified – as in a picture of peas on a packet of frozen peas), or *conventional* (where the sign is merely invented, the result of an agreement or convention – like the colour red being a sign of danger in Western societies). Peirce called these last signs "symbols".

THEY ARE THE ODDEST BECAUSE THEY ARE CONSTITUTED MERELY BY THE FACT THAT THEY ARE USED OR UNDERSTOOD AS SUCH.

Words and language are constructed out of such symbols. Natural and iconic signs usually signal the presence of that which they refer to. But symbols like words rarely do so. If I read a book with the symbol "elephant" in it, I rarely infer from this that there are any in my house. So Peirce was getting very close to the fact that words are "arbitrary" symbols which somehow still generate meaning, and the ramifications of this discovery are very serious for philosophy, as we shall see in the last section of this book.

WILLIAM JAMES

William James was greatly influenced by Peirce's Pragmatism. James agreed that ideas should not be seen as abstract metaphysical entities but tools with practical uses – like the ability to predict experiences. His book **The Principles of Psychology** (1890) is the first real textbook on the subject of the human mind in which it was insisted that psychology should be more like one of the experimental natural sciences. James was interested in the physical basis of consciousness and its biological function, which he explained in Darwinian terms.

HUMAN EVOLUTION IS AN INTERACTIVE PROCESS IN WHICH CONSCIOUSNESS AND THE ENVIRONMENT INFLUENCE EACH OTHER – CONSCIOUSNESS EXISTS IN ORDER TO ENABLE US TO SURVIVE.

Jamesian psychology is often known as Functionalism – it is what consciousness does and the differences it makes that he saw as its important features. James also recognized how consciousness exists as a continuous flow rather than as a series of discrete ideas – an insight which influenced both 20th century fiction and the Phenomenology of Husserl. James also thought it was possible to exercise free-will in order to cure oneself of depression, something he himself did. He noticed that religious belief often gave meaning to the lives of many individuals and in his later life he studied the phenomena of mysticism in **The Varieties of Religious Experience** (1902). He finally came to believe that God exists, but is finite, which rather neatly explains how and why human beings are free and separate from God, and why evil exists in the world.

JOHN DEWEY

John Dewey (1859-1952) was a systematic pragmatist or "instrumentalist" who believed that being "philosophical" really meant being critically intelligent and maintaining a "scientific" approach to human problems. Pragmatists like Dewey were great enthusiasts for the successes of science and its methods of inquiry. Dewey was convinced that philosophy could also play a key role in a creative American democracy by contributing to all kinds of knowledge in ethics, art, education, and the newly emerging social sciences. Like Peirce, Dewey was a theoretical "fallibilist", but still firmly a believer in the real possibility of practical progress in human affairs. Society can only progress if its members are educated to be intelligent and flexible.

I PROPOSE THAT EDUCATIONALISTS SHOULD NO LONGER CONCEIVE OF CHILDREN AS PASSIVE, EMPTY JAMJARS WHO NEED TO BE STUFFED WITH INFORMATION.

BUT AS INDEPENDENTLY-MINDED PROBLEM-SOLVERS WHO NEED TO BE CONTINUALLY CHALLENGED.

In his famous Laboratory School at the University of Chicago, children were (and still are) encouraged to solve problems by inventing hypotheses and testing them. Dewey thought that art should be encouraged because it stimulates imaginative "solutions" to its own unique "problems".

DEMOCRACY

Dewey approved of democracy for very pragmatic reasons. Democratic societies are best because they are flexible, avoid dogma, and so can cope with change. This also meant that Dewey was interested in the new discipline of Sociology because of its ability to produce useful statistics. Social problems, he thought, could not be solved with abstract theorizing.

THERE ARE NO GENUINE THEORIES OF HISTORY AND SOCIETY, ONLY DETAILED CONCRETE ANALYSES.

Like all of us, Dewey was a product of his time. His vision of "society" is limited to a rather middle-class, small-town American viewpoint and his views are gradualist. Education rather than agitation is what he thought would improve the lives of ordinary Americans.

NEO-PRAGMATISTS

In post-war America, Pragmatism was eventually eclipsed by the European imports of analytic philosophy and phenomenology, but not for long. Pragmatism never really disappeared. American philosophers still believe that their subject has to be of some practical use, although there is a lot of disagreement about what exactly that use might be. One American philosopher, **W.V. Quine** (b. 1908), almost single-handedly showed that some of the central dogmas of analytic philosophy are in fact worryingly imprecise. He is a pragmatist because he suggests that human knowledge is inevitably **holistic**.

KNOWLEDGE IS A "MATRIX" OR INTEGRATED BODY OF BELIEFS WHICH CAN ALWAYS BE CHANGED BY EXPERIENCE – EVEN OUR "BELIEFS" IN MATHS AND LOGIC.

I AM PROFOUNDLY SUSPICIOUS OF "FOUNDATIONAL" PHILOSOPHY WHICH SUGGESTS THERE IS SOME SPECIAL WAY IN WHICH PHILOSOPHERS CAN LOCATE UNQUESTIONABLE TRUTHS ABOUT REALITY OR ESTABLISH "FOUNDATIONS" FOR ALL HUMAN KNOWLEDGE.

Another American philosopher, **Richard Rorty** (b. 1931), is often labelled as a "sophisticated neo-pragmatist", partly because he still insists on asking what philosophy is actually for.

113

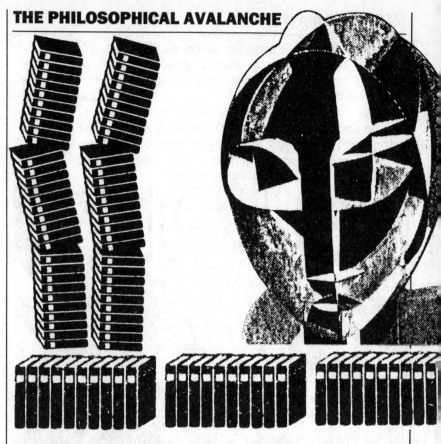

There are now at least 10,000 professional academic philosophers in the United States. They still conceive of philosophy as a practical activity that is dealing with the "problems" of consciousness and artificial intelligence, medical ethics, human rights, mathematics, the implications of epistemological and ethical relativism, logic, and so on. American philosophy is a vast and industrious enterprise which this small book can only summarize very inadequately.

John Rawls (b. 1921) in **A Theory of Justice** has tried to show how it is possible to reconcile social justice with a liberal capitalist democracy with an ingenious fictional pre-societal contract.

Saul Kripke (b. 1940) has tried to change the way philosophers think about the relationship between logic and experience. He claims that our knowledge that water is H_2O is as "certain" as our knowledge of maths and logic.

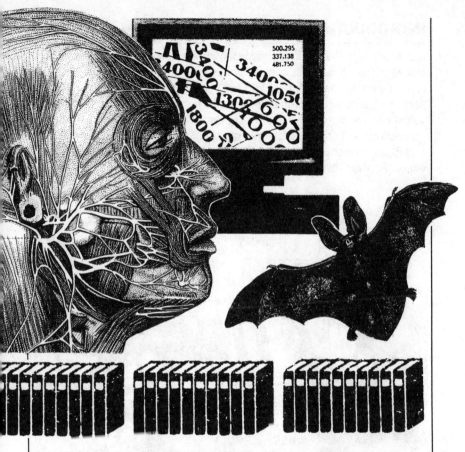

Daniel Dennett (b. 1942) has produced radical new ideas about the nature of human consciousness, as has **Thomas Nagel** (b. 1937) in his famous essay entitled **What Is It Like to Be a Bat?**.

John Searle (b. 1932) has produced work on the philosophy of language and is critical of all enthusiastic materialist theories of mind. He maintains that number-crunching computers will always be faster but more stupid than us because they can have no convincing grasp of "meaning".

The neo-pragmatic Rorty notoriously maintains that philosophy is no more than one entertaining voice in a vast general civilized conversation, or worse, a kind of "illness" for which its practitioners need therapy. This sceptical view may well be true, but it seems very unlikely to stem the frightening number of new American philosophical books and articles now published every year (about 4,000).

INTRODUCTION TO 20TH CENTURY PHILOSOPHY

Nietzsche said that philosophical ideas are no more than the dominant beliefs of their time. 20th century philosophy is no exception to this rule. Its philosophers tend in different ways to address the same dominant themes, such as problems of modern mass society, loss of individual identity, doubt and relativist uncertainty. The focus is also more specialized on complex problems of human consciousness, meaning and logic. Philosophy of the last eighty years is often categorized as either "Analytic" or "Continental".

ANALYTIC PHILOSOPHY IS USUALLY BRITISH OR AMERICAN ...

CONTINENTAL IS MOSTLY FRENCH AND GERMAN.

BUT, CONFUSINGLY, THE TWO GREATEST ANALYTIC PHILOSOPHERS, FREGE AND WITTGENSTEIN, WERE GERMAN AND AUSTRIAN.

Continental philosophy might be characterized as re-thinking the tradition established by Descartes, Kant and Hegel.

ORIGINS OF PHENOMENOLOGY

Kant's criticism of metaphysics had concluded that all we can ever know with any degree of empirical certainty is the phenomenal world of sense experience, the state of appearances, but never the noumenal world of things as they "really are". The question could be asked: "But what is it that we are experiencing when we experience?"

Phenomenology launched an attempt to answer that question by focusing on the analysis of how things appear to the consciousness.

Franz Brentano (1838-1917), philosopher and psychologist, proposed a "descriptive or phenomenal psychology".

*I WANT TO KNOW EXACTLY **WHAT** IT IS THAT THE INDIVIDUAL KNOWS WHEN PRESENTED WITH SOMETHING IN HIS CONSCIOUSNESS.*

Brentano insisted on the primacy of **intention**: consciousness always has an "intentional" object, it is always directed *at* something. If I believe, hate or see, then there is always something that I believe, hate or see – even if it doesn't actually exist, like a ghost or memory.

117

LINKS TO PSYCHOLOGY AND MATHEMATICS

Phenomenology is directly linked to the birth of experimental psychology, officially founded in 1879 by **Wilhelm Wundt** (1832-1920). He was the first to propose that **introspection** – the examination of one's own mental states according to strict rules – could be an experimental method. Brentano himself was close to a founder of Gestalt psychology, **Christian von Ehrenfels** (1859-1932). Mathematics also provided an important link in the case of **Edmund Husserl** (1859-1938), originally a philosopher of mathematics, who adopted Brentano's idea of intentional consciousness. He defined Phenomenology as a description of the *content* of consciousness.

THE ONLY ROUTE TO TRUE KNOWLEDGE LIES IN THE EXAMINATION OF ONE'S OWN CONSCIOUSNESS.

I AGREE, MONSIEUR DESCARTES, BUT HOW CAN YOU BE SURE WHAT CONSCIOUSNESS ACTUALLY IS?

THE METHOD OF REDUCTIONS

There seemed only one way to know for sure what consciousness is. This was to perform a series of "reductions" which ignore all metaphysical and theoretical distractions so as to concentrate solely on the contents of consciousness and its essential feature of "intentionality". Husserl called this *epoche* or suspension.

THE TRICK IS TO SUSPEND OR "BRACKET" ALL QUESTIONS OF "TRUTH" OR "REALITY", SO THAT ONLY THE UNIQUE PURE IMMEDIACY OF EXPERIENCE REMAINS AS CONTENT.

The problem is, as Husserl recognized, that such an exercise will lead to **solipsism** – all you can be fully certain of is *yourself*. And he had doubts even about this, since our identity is never directly present in our consciousness.

HEIDEGGER: THE QUEST FOR BEING

Phenomenology reached out to a primordial level of consciousness. The question was: are "things themselves" perceived in consciousness, or is the world only there *for* a mind? **Martin Heidegger** (1889-1976), a student of Husserl, radicalized the question by asking even more fundamentally what it means *to be*. This question of Being, called "fundamental ontology" in Heidegger's **Being and Time** (1927), concerns us decisively as existing human beings.

WHAT IS "IS"?
IF WE FORGET THIS BASIC QUESTION OF BEING, WE LOSE SIGHT OF THE WAY **WE ARE** IN THE WORLD.

Descartes' notion that "I am" by "thinking I am", just like Husserl's identity of consciousness, forgets that I exist by mortal constraint in this world. "Being there" in the world (*Dasein*) is not at all the same as "being conscious". Human beingness is our ability to exist in the world, determined by the choices we make, including false or inauthentic ones.

NOTHINGNESS AND INAUTHENTICITY

Heidegger asks: "Why is there anything rather than nothing?" We confront an anxiety without object, a "nothingness" (*Das Nichts*) which is our own oncoming death. But while we live, our being in this world must be realized by acts of free choice. Only this can give us some guarantee of **authenticity**. We are "thrown" into the world, and for most people this will mean being determined by "them", by the average everyday roles others impose on us.

> *THE ROLE WE ASSUME MAKES US **INAUTHENTIC** BECAUSE IT IS NOT OWNED BY US.*

But is it possible to be "self-authentic" in a time of mass society, totalitarian ideologies and technology? In view of the difficulties, Heidegger concluded that human beings need to commit themselves to their own culture and traditions – a standpoint which led him to make his own disastrous political choice of supporting Hitler and Nazism, something which he seems never to have regretted. He thus remains a problematic figure.

121

SARTRE'S EXISTENTIALISM

Heidegger denied any connection to **Existentialism**, a philosophy chiefly developed by **Jean-Paul Sartre** (1905-80) from typically Continental sources: Descartes, Hegel and Husserl. Although Sartre's **Being and Nothingness** (1943) is clearly influenced by Heidegger, finally Marx is more important. Sartre was also in search of "authenticity" and he shared Kierkegaard's belief in "commitment". But everything crucially depends on the fact that there is no God, which makes the universe "absurd", without meaning or purpose. No God also means no such thing as "human nature", because human beings have not been "manufactured" to some divine plan or "essence".

SO, WE ARE ALL CONDEMNED TO FREEDOM AND MUST CHOOSE FOR OURSELVES **WHO** WE ARE.

ONE IS NOT BORN A WOMAN.

We are "self made" by choice, or as Sartre says, "existence precedes essence". Hence, the name Existentialism.

FREEDOM AND BAD FAITH

In many ways, Sartre's Existentialism is very Cartesian. Mind is all we can be certain of. He always contrasts the freedom and imagination of our human consciousness with non-conscious, non-free objects like paper-knives. But for Sartre the "self" is not some static phenomenon we discover through Cartesian self-examination. It is a personal project for which we have to take responsibility.

NO ONE CAN JUSTIFIABLY SAY "I AM A NATURALLY LAZY PERSON", BECAUSE THEY HAVE **CHOSEN** TO BE LAZY. THIS IS AN EXAMPLE OF **BAD FAITH**.

THE FREEDOM TO CHOOSE WHO I AM IS A FRIGHTENING THOUGHT.

People of "bad faith" will try to escape it in all sorts of ways, often by slipping into a social role ("I am a waiter, that's who I am."). They become like **things** – but they also confirm the reality of freedom. But is freedom really so "total" as Sartre makes out? And is "bad faith" always so bad?

AUTHENTIC POLITICAL LIFE

We can see why authentic choice was such a real issue for Sartre. The Nazi Occupation forces entered Paris in 1941. Everyone had to decide whether just to get by, collaborate with the Nazis, or fight. Sartre joined the Resistance. Later in life he supported Algerian independence and refused the Nobel Prize. He always claimed that Marxism was the only valid philosophy for the modern world.

EXISTENTIALISM CANNOT REPLACE MARXISM. ALL IT CAN DO IS HUMANIZE MARXISM AND SAFEGUARD IT FROM THE CRIMES COMMITTED IN ITS NAME BY STALIN.

Sartre engaged all his life in a fight against his own personal "inauthenticity", so as not to slip into the easy role of "the famous Existentialist philosopher".

CAMUS AND THE ABSURD

Albert Camus (1913-60), born in Algeria, a journalist, essayist and novelist, also denied being an Existentialist. But his exploration of the emotional significance of what it means to live in a godless "absurd universe" certainly contributed to it. His commitment to the French Resistance brought him close to Sartre, but they disagreed sharply on the issues of Communism and Algeria's independence. How can you affirm meaning in a meaningless universe? Camus illustrates this in **The Myth of Sisyphus** (1943). Sisyphus was condemned by the gods to push a rock uphill, which then rolls down again, and so on, forever. Camus begins his book with a question …

> THERE IS BUT ONE TRULY SERIOUS PHILOSOPHICAL PROBLEM, AND THAT IS SUICIDE.

… and he continues: "Judging whether life is or is not worth living amounts to answering the fundamental question of philosophy." Sisyphus defiantly chooses to give his useless task a meaning, and it thereby acquires a meaning. So also must human beings do in their own "absurd" lives.

125

ANALYTICAL PHILOSOPHY:
THE PROBLEM OF MATHEMATICS

Philosophers do have this annoying habit of asking very simple questions which often have appallingly difficult answers. Everyone knows that two plus two equals four. But philosophers ask **why**. Pythagoras was convinced that mathematics was the key to the understanding of everything. Plato believed that numbers had some kind of separate mystical existence. One of the chief preoccupations of some 20th century "analytic" philosophers has been the attempt to find the "foundations" of mathematics in **logic**.

MATHEMATICS SEEMS TO OFFER A SPECIAL KIND OF GUARANTEED KNOWLEDGE.

TWO AND TWO ALWAYS MAKE FOUR AND THIS "NECESSARY TRUTH" CAN NEVER BE DOUBTED.

This annoyed the Victorian empiricist philosopher John Stuart Mill, who thought mathematical certainty seemed too much like a "free lunch". He claimed that mathematics is just a highly probable inductive truth, based on our human experience of the world.

WE KNOW THAT 3+3 = 6 FROM OUR OBSERVATIONS OF THINGS GROUPED IN THREES.

BUT MOST PHILOSOPHERS THINK THIS IS WRONG.

WE BELIEVE THAT MATHEMATICS IS "A PRIORI" – A **SELF-CONTAINED** SYSTEM WHICH IS **ALWAYS** TRUE, REGARDLESS OF HUMAN BEINGS AND THEIR WORLD.

But if this is true, why does mathematics often give us an accurate picture of how the universe works? Kant's explanation was that mathematics was another example of the "synthetic a priori" – mathematics is always true for us, because that is the way our brains are "wired up".

FREGE AND DEMYSTIFIED MATHS

Gottlob Frege (1848-1925) lived a secluded and uneventful life, but changed Western philosophy forever by making logic the foundation of modern philosophy instead of "the problem of knowledge". He jettisoned traditional deductive logic and produced a new "formal" and "symbolic" version. By using this new logic he thought he could demonstrate the deep connections between mathematics and logic. Frege demystified mathematics by showing that numbers aren't "objects" like giraffes.

NUMBERS ARE THE "PROPERTIES OF CONCEPTS" OR USEFUL LOGICAL FICTIONS – RATHER LIKE THE FICTION OF "THE AVERAGE MAN".

Frege then showed how mathematics is analytic or "empty".

SO 2+2 = 4 IS A "TAUTOLOGY" –
NO MORE THAN 1+1+1+1 = 1+1+1+1 –
NOTHING TO DO WITH OUR
OBSERVATIONS OF THE WORLD OR
HOW OUR MINDS ARE
CONSTRUCTED.

Rationalist philosophers have often advanced mathematics as the greatest paradigm of the sorts of fundamental truths produced by reason. Frege's demystifying account of mathematical knowledge is crucial because it helped to destroy the illusion that there was some kind of special metaphysical knowledge that only philosophers could discover.

THE MYSTERY REMAINS

Frege seems to have come very close to solving the philosophical problem of mathematical truth. Unfortunately, in 1903, Bertrand Russell discovered a paradox which seems unresolvable in the Frege system, and **Kurt Gödel** (1906-78) showed that there will always be mathematical truths which remain unprovable in any self-consistent logical system. Any formal system can be consistent or complete, but not both.

IN ANY SYSTEM CONTAINING ARITHMETIC, THERE ARE TRUE STATEMENTS WHICH CANNOT BE PROVED WITHIN THE SYSTEM.

So mathematics still escapes from logic and remains one of the central problems of modern philosophy.

MEANING AND REFERENCE

Frege is also one of the founders of modern linguistic philosophy. He helped to change the agenda of modern philosophy from the problem of knowledge to the even more fundamental one of **meaning**. Frege stressed that everyday grammatical language is not logical and that logic itself is independent of psychology. Language itself has two different functions.

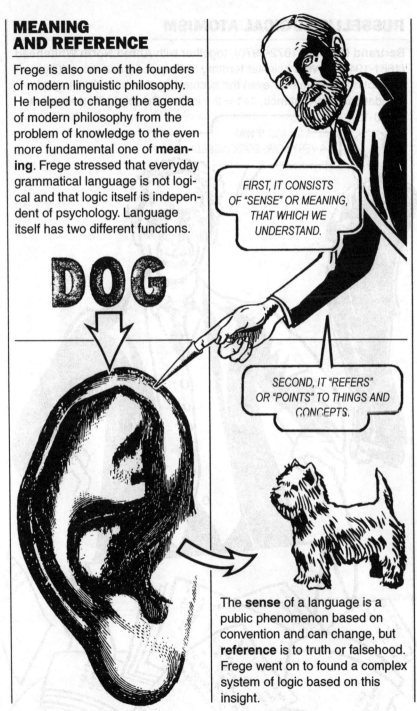

FIRST, IT CONSISTS OF "SENSE" OR MEANING, THAT WHICH WE UNDERSTAND.

SECOND, IT "REFERS" OR "POINTS" TO THINGS AND CONCEPTS.

The **sense** of a language is a public phenomenon based on convention and can change, but **reference** is to truth or falsehood. Frege went on to found a complex system of logic based on this insight.

RUSSELL'S LOGICAL ATOMISM

Bertrand Russell (1872-1970), together with **Alfred North Whitehead** (1861-1947), covered similar territory to Frege's by unsuccessfully attempting to prove how even the simplest mathematics had logical foundations – for instance, 1+1 = 2 – in their **Principia Mathematica** (1910-13).

AND IT WAS A VERY LONG BOOK INDEED!

In the respectable traditions of English empiricism, Russell was a "logical atomist". He thought that the best way to understand the world is to split everything down into individual components. Individual propositions can then be shown to refer to individual sensations in the mind, themselves caused by individual "bits" of the world.

WE CAN ONLY BE CERTAIN OF THE THINGS WE KNOW BY **DIRECT ACQUAINTANCE**.

EVERYTHING ELSE MUST BE BUILT UP BY **LOGICAL CONSTRUCTION** FROM THIS BASIC DATA.

Ordinary language must be broken down into its logical form, if it is ever to be unambiguous. A good example of how this works is the "is" word. Russell proposed what he called a theory of "definite descriptions", using the famous example: "The king of France is bald." What is the "is" describing here? Russell tackles the "is" strictly by logical analysis, totally unlike Heidegger's "being", as we'll now see.

LOGICAL ANALYSIS

The sentence "The king of France is bald" is odd because it seems to refer to someone who doesn't exist. Russell's solution to this linguistic puzzle is to break the ordinary sentence into its logical components, so it is easier to see where things have gone wrong, like this ...

▷ THERE EXISTS A "PRESENT" KING OF FRANCE. **WRONG**

▷ EVERYTHING WHICH IS A KING OF FRANCE IS BALD.

▷ THERE IS ONLY ONE KING OF FRANCE.

So the "is" of the original sentence, "The king of France is bald", slyly implies that a king exists when he *doesn't*, and logical analysis reveals this clearly. This kind of analysis also reveals the difference between the "sense" of a sentence and its "reference".

Both Frege and Russell thought that modern philosophy could no longer have a subject matter but would have to become an "analytic activity". 20th century philosophers would have to be logicians, not clairvoyants delving into "the innermost nature of reality". This didn't stop Russell, an English Lord, from pontificating on a large number of moral and political issues during his lifetime.

THE LOGICAL POSITIVISTS

The Logical Positivists – or the "Vienna Circle" – were social and physical scientists rather than philosophers. **Moritz Schlick** (1882-1936), **Otto Neurath** (1882-1945) and **Rudolf Carnap** (1891-1970) thought that all philosophy, especially Hegelian idealism, was metaphysical nonsense.

FOR US, MEANING AND TESTABILITY ARE THE SAME THING.

*WE DEVISED THE "VERIFICATION PRINCIPLE" WHICH DECLARES THAT ANY PROPOSITION THAT CANNOT BE **TESTED** EMPIRICALLY IS NONSENSE.*

SO "GOD IS ABSOLUTE AND ETERNAL" LOOKS LIKE SENSE, BUT IS WHOLLY UNTESTABLE AND THEREFORE GIBBERISH.

They thought that the "surface grammar" of language had led philosophers into endless, unsolvable pseudo-debates about imaginary entities like the "substances" of Spinoza and Leibniz.

A.J. AYER'S LOGICAL POSITIVISM

The Logical Positivists thought that there was no such thing as "philosophical knowledge" – the road to real knowledge was only through science. Philosophy could only be an analytic activity which clarified concepts and cleared up linguistic confusions. **A.J. Ayer** (1910-89) went to Vienna to see them in the 1930s and returned to England as a disciple. He wrote his book **Language, Truth and Logic** when he was twenty-six, and its cool technical dismissal of both religion and ethical language as "nonsense" shocked some members of the British establishment.

LOGICAL POSITIVISM, FAR FROM BEING A FOREIGN IMPORT, IS JUST A RADICAL RESTATEMENT OF TRADITIONAL ENGLISH EMPIRICISM.

TESTING FOR MEANING

The individual members of the Vienna Circle, all believers in tolerance and scientific progress, eventually had to flee from the insanities of Nazi Germany. Schlick was shot dead by one of his deranged students, something philosophy teachers usually like to keep quiet about.

As a theory of meaning, **verificationism** collapsed fairly quickly, partly because a lot of modern science is conceptual and untestable in a simple "look and see" way. No one has ever seen a "quark", so how could such a thing be "tested"? Meaning also has to be prior to testing, not a result of it. How can we test something if we don't understand it first? It was left to another Viennese philosopher to sort out this problem of meaning more convincingly.

WITTGENSTEIN'S LOGICAL ATOMISM

Ludwig Wittgenstein (1889-1951) at first studied engineering. His interest in the logic of mathematics led him to work with Bertrand Russell at Cambridge in 1911. He was from a rich, talented but tragic Viennese family – three of his brothers committed suicide. He was a charismatic, impatient and enigmatic teacher who came to reject the academic teaching of philosophy as useless, a privately religious man who changed Western philosophy forever. He served in the Austrian army in World War I.

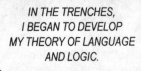

IN THE TRENCHES, I BEGAN TO DEVELOP MY THEORY OF LANGUAGE AND LOGIC.

He published a short, intensely difficult work,

the **Tractatus Logico-Philosophicus**, in 1922.

The **Tractatus** begins with these words: "The world is all that is the case." Wittgenstein at first adopted Russell's "atomism", which insists that sentences must be "broken down" to reveal their logical complexities. He attempted to show that meaning ultimately derives from atomic logical sentences which form an accurate "picture" of what he puzzlingly called the "atomic facts" of the world.

THE LIMITS OF MY LANGUAGE ARE THE LIMITS OF MY WORLD.

This premise means that there are limits to the sorts of meaningful thoughts that we can have with language. Metaphysical problems only arise because philosophers are always trying to "say what cannot be said". So does the book end: "Of what we cannot speak we must remain silent."

THE MEANING OF MEANING

Wittgenstein subsequently abandoned his first "atomist" attempt to solve the "problem of meaning" and began to question all traditional philosophical quests for generality or "essences". This new, very different approach was **descriptive** thinking, eventually published in a posthumous book, **Philosophical Investigations** (1953).

THE GREAT 20TH CENTURY SEARCH FOR THE "MEANING OF MEANING" IS FUTILE BECAUSE IT IS FOUNDED ON THE MISCONCEPTION THAT "MEANING" IS SOMETHING "SEPARATE" FROM LANGUAGE.

This is not a philosopher.

So, just because there is a useful word for the concept of Art, there is no point in going on a search for "the one essential thing" that gives the word "Art" meaning, or asking how the concept exists in the mind. The word "Art" is just used by people to refer to many different activities and artefacts that share "family resemblances".

LANGUAGE GAMES

Language is a series of different kinds of "games" with many different purposes and goals. Meaning is the result of socially agreed conventions produced by "forms of life" and cannot possibly be established "outside" of language. This means that language is autonomous and floats free of the world. Wittgenstein adopted a therapeutic view of philosophical discourse, which he thought was a kind of sickness – the product of a language "going on a holiday", so that one language game became confused with another.

THERAPY GAMES LIFE

LANGUAGE

OUTSIDE

FORMS OF

MEANING

GAMES

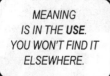

MEANING
IS IN THE **USE**.
YOU WON'T FIND IT
ELSEWHERE.

PRIVATE THOUGHTS

Wittgenstein's later philosophy of mind is also anti-Cartesian. Thought is **linguistic**. Language is a social product and therefore consciousness cannot be "private". This means that any phenomenological "first person" quest for "certainty" is misconceived. Descartes and his numerous philosopher-disciples always contended that first person experiences are somehow more "immediate" and certain than other kinds. But to talk or write about mental experiences means using a **public** language with socially agreed rules which lay down both meanings and references.

FREUD'S THEORY OF THE UNCONSCIOUS

Wittgenstein's "therapy" solution to philosophy's linguistic illness owes something to another Viennese, **Sigmund Freud** (1856-1939), the founder of psychoanalysis. Freud's hugely influential theory of a sexually structured **unconscious** emerged from neurophysiology and clinical practice. But the notion that we are often "unconscious" of our own mental processes was already known to 19th century philosophers like Schopenhauer. Freud went further to propose that civilization itself is only made possible by the repression of the sexual drive at an unconscious level, a view which undermines the philosophical quest for objective rationality.

HUMAN BEINGS REMAIN IGNORANT OF THE PRIMITIVE ORIGINS OF THEIR THOUGHTS, BELIEFS AND DESIRES.

THE UNCONSCIOUS IS A FICTION. SOMETHING CANNOT BE BOTH "UNCONSCIOUS" AND "MENTAL" AT THE SAME TIME.

Jean-Paul Sartre is one among other philosophers and psychologists who dismissed Freud's unconscious as empirically unverifiable.

ORDINARY LANGUAGE PHILOSOPHY

Wittgenstein thought that it was the modern philosopher's therapeutic job to "show the fly the way out of the flybottle" – or show how most philosophical puzzles were just the result of linguistic confusion.

J.L. Austin (1911-60), the Oxford don of "ordinary language" philosophy, opened many more linguistic "flybottles". The point was to examine in detail how ideas like "perception" or "knowledge" are used in ordinary language. Austin introduced the concept of **performative speech-acts**. In brief, this means that we do not only *say* something, but *do* something. If I say to someone, "It looks like rain", I am performing a series of acts.

*I DON'T MEAN THAT "LOOKS" IS ITSELF A REAL ENTITY – BUT I AM **WARNING** YOU ABOUT THE RAIN AND **ADVISING** YOU TO TAKE AN UMBRELLA.*

THE GHOST IN THE MACHINE

Gilbert Ryle (1900-76), another influential Oxford philosopher, also arrived at a parallel view of "ordinary concepts" via British empiricism and an interest in the Phenomenology of Brentano and Husserl. Philosophers often commit what Ryle called "category mistakes" in **The Concept of Mind** (1949). The notorious example is Descartes' myth of a disembodied mind having private thoughts, like a "ghost in the machine".

*SUCH TALK ABOUT "INNER PRIVATE EXPERIENCES" SHOULD ALWAYS BE ENVISAGED AS **DISPOSITIONS** TO BEHAVE A CERTAIN WAY.*

Ryle took a philosophically **behaviourist** view that mental terms must always translate into physical sensations. This behaviourist view of language and meaning might be convincing if all talk about sensations and thoughts always referred to those of other people. It remains unconvincing as an account of how we use language to refer to our own thoughts and beliefs.

THE PHILOSOPHY OF SCIENCE

A division between "continental" and "analytic" philosophies – which, as we have seen, is far from definite – is in any case less important than the acknowledgement that science seems to rule supreme in the 20th century. Scientists, not philosophers, have changed how we live, our knowledge of the world and our views about ourselves.

BUT WHY IS SCIENTIFIC KNOWLEDGE SO SPECIAL?

AND HOW DOES IT DIFFER FROM OTHER KINDS OF KNOWLEDGE?

It is easy to be blinded by all this success and become prey to "Scientism" – the worship of science and a naïve belief that it can solve all of our human problems.

There are all sorts of scientists. Some wear white coats and use expensive-looking technical equipment, others just write impenetrable mathematical stuff on blackboards. But it is commonly believed that they are all "scientists" because they employ some kind of special scientific "method" which produces a unique **kind** of knowledge. Scientific knowledge is usually thought to be "universal", "quantifiable", "empirical" and with "predictive power". A frog scientist should be able to tell us something about **all** frogs.

THE INDUCTION METHOD

So, where do scientists get their theories from? Induction is one obvious scientific "method". A scientist observes and measures lots of swimming and walking frogs under different conditions and finally produces an "amphibian theory". But over two hundred years ago, the philosopher Hume pointed out that induction offers only probability and not certainty.

> THE SCIENTIST CAN ONLY EVER SAY THAT IT IS ONLY **PROBABLE SO FAR** THAT ALL FROGS ARE AMPHIBIOUS.

But is seeing **proving**? What we "see" is often influenced by our cultural and educational conditioning. It is difficult to escape from all of our presuppositions about the world, and equally impossible to describe what we see in a language that is "objective".

Seeing isn't just a process of passively receiving sensory data, but a much more complex process of receiving, selecting and categorizing information.

THIS MEANS THAT ANY OBSERVATION, EVEN OF FROGS, IS BOUND TO BE "THEORY-LADEN".

Our scientist will undoubtedly have certain presuppositions about what frogs are, what swimming involves, how many he needs to count, and so on, before he emerges with his new theory. Any science based on induction will never be certain, and will always have a problem with its human and questionable "empirical base".

FALSIFICATION THEORY

Karl Popper (1902-94) suggested that "Falsification Theory" would be a more sensible way of thinking about scientific procedure. In his view, scientific theories must always be provisional. True scientists will always suggest ways in which their theories could be "falsified" by some new contradictory observation.

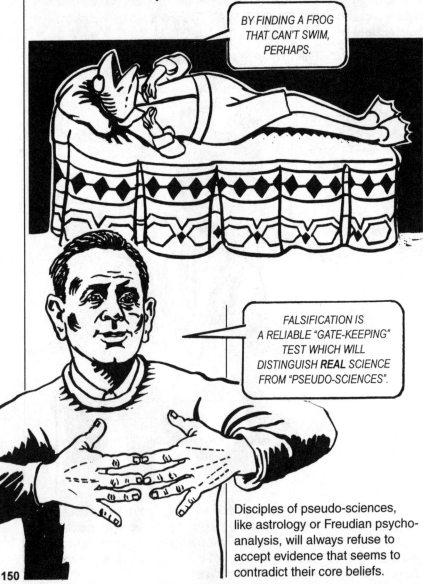

BY FINDING A FROG THAT CAN'T SWIM, PERHAPS.

*FALSIFICATION IS A RELIABLE "GATE-KEEPING" TEST WHICH WILL DISTINGUISH **REAL** SCIENCE FROM "PSEUDO-SCIENCES".*

Disciples of pseudo-sciences, like astrology or Freudian psycho-analysis, will always refuse to accept evidence that seems to contradict their core beliefs.

But as a scientific method, falsificationism has its own problems. If our observations of the world are themselves always "theory-laden", why should one observation immediately invalidate a complex scientific theory? How do we know which to trust? Scientific theories are complex and interdependent, so it is not always easy to falsify them with a single observation. History also reveals that scientists have often been very reluctant to jettison their pet theories because of one contradictory observation. Sometimes they have been quite right to be stubborn – but not always.

Max Planck (1858-1947) is an interesting case. Quantum physics begins with Planck's mathematical discovery which seemed to violate the sacrosanct Second Law of Thermodynamics.

I EXHAUSTED MYSELF FOR YEARS TRYING TO REFUTE MY OWN REVOLUTIONARY INSIGHT INTO MATTER AND RADIATION ...

THOMAS KUHN: THE PARADIGM SHIFT

For Popper, science is like an erratic but systematic escalator powered by reason which gradually progresses towards an accumulation of scientific "truth". **Thomas Kuhn** (b. 1922) challenged this naïvely progressivist view of science. He looked closely at the history of science and asked: how does any community of scientists actually practise its branch of science?

ARISTOTLE

COPERNICUS

NEWTON

*IT BECOMES EVIDENT THAT ONE PARTICULAR THEORY OR **PARADIGM** IS ALWAYS TAKEN FOR GRANTED AS THE RIGHT WAY TO EXAMINE THE WORLD.*

But paradigms radically change or "shift" in the course of history. Cosmological paradigms have been variously Aristotelian, Ptolemaic, Copernican and Newtonian, and are currently Einsteinian.

So, why do paradigms change? Because a paradigm will accumulate unsolved puzzles, not "truth", which arise from the challenges posed by scientists themselves. The claims of Galileo or Einstein brought the dominant paradigms of their times into crisis.

Scientific belief systems about heavenly spheres or light rays will then just collapse, unable to accommodate new ideas. Kuhn insists that science "progresses" through sudden revolutionary changes, and not by some methodical evolutionary process. Scientific belief isn't *that* different from religious faith. New science gets accepted, not because of the persuasive force of striking new evidence, but because old scientists die off and young ones replace them.

EPISTEMOLOGICAL ANARCHISM

Scientists felt that Kuhn was threatening the rationality and progress of science, which is not the case. But perhaps the most radical critic of science remains the Austrian-born **Paul Feyerabend** (1924-94). His account of the growth of science in **Against Method** (1974) stresses a plurality of competing theories, or what he called "epistemological anarchism".

IF SCIENCE CAN BE SAID TO "PROGRESS" AT ALL, IT'S THANKS TO THE MAVERICK SCIENTISTS WHO ACTED AGAINST THE ESTABLISHED METHODS.

It is foolish to expect that "science" – which is creative by being inherently pluralist and anarchistic – can be governed by any discoverable fixed set of methodological rules. Moreover, there is nothing fundamentally "superior" about scientific knowledge.

FROM MODERN TO POSTMODERN

Modern philosophy begins with Descartes' attempt to discover an assured and realizable truth, an **empirical foundation**, no matter how much of "reality" had to be sacrificed in the process. For him, this foundation must be the **cogito** – "I think therefore I am."

THIS IS THE ABSOLUTE MINIMUM WHICH WILL GUARANTEE OBJECTIVE SCIENTIFIC TRUTH, BASED ON THE REALITY OF THE THINKING SELF.

BUT WHAT HAPPENS IF YOUR "FOUNDATION" COLLAPSES UNDER PHILOSOPHICAL SCRUTINY?

Doubts concerning the existence of the self, objective truth and the meaning of language have escalated since Descartes into an identifiable "crisis" of knowledge, now called the postmodern condition.

THE THREE BIG "IFS" OF POSTMODERNISM

We can perhaps best understand postmodern philosophy as haunted by three big "ifs".

If human thoughts can no longer be guaranteed as "ours" …

If the language we think with cannot meaningfully refer to the world outside itself …

If the meanings of autonomous linguistic signs are constantly shifting …

Then, it's very bad news for philosophy, logic and even science itself.

The key to postmodern scepticism is the problem of language, or rather, the illusion of its meaning.

NIETZSCHE: THE DELUSION OF TRUTH

The seeds of postmodernist scepticism have always been present within Western philosophy, ever since Cratylus who refused to speak because he considered the meanings of his words to be unstable. One more obvious and recent founding father of postmodernism is Nietzsche, who insisted that language could only ever be metaphorical.

WHAT ARE MAN'S TRUTHS ULTIMATELY? MERELY HIS IRREFUTABLE ERRORS.

LOGIC RELIES ON THE DOMINANT TENDENCY TO TREAT AS EQUAL WHAT IS MERELY SIMILAR ... NOTHING IS REALLY EQUAL.

Nietzsche thought that what counted as "knowledge" was simply that which the strongest imposed on everyone else. *Let us guard against the dangerous fiction that posited a painless, timeless, knowing "subject", the snares of such contradictory concepts as "pure reason" or "knowledge in itself".*

LANGUAGE AND REALITY

Postmodern scepticism is not merely a whim but an inevitable consequence of history. We have seen a lot of complicated arguments about language, meaning and knowledge in our journey through Western philosophy. Here are three very different modern philosophers, Heidegger, Wittgenstein and Jacques Derrida, who have doubts about the relationship of language to reality.

What are they really saying? **Heidegger**: as human beings, we can never separate language and reality. **Wittgenstein**: there are only localized "language games" of which Western philosophy is one example. **Derrida**: we use language to think and communicate with, but we can have no objective way of knowing what its relationship is to any reality "outside" it. Our thoughts are "trapped" in it.

A SYSTEM OF SIGNS

Ferdinand de Saussure (1857-1913), a Swiss linguist, was the founder of structuralism and semiology. He gave up the search for the "meaning" of language and instead opted for a description of its **use** function. Linguistic "meaning" does not derive from correspondence to things "out there" but from relations between signs themselves and their positions within a system of signifiers.

QUEEN OF DIAMONDS

Gambling PALACE

HOT SHOT

LANGUAGE'S RELATION TO THE WORLD IS **ARBITRARY**. IT DOES NOT SIGNIFY REALITY.

Or as Saussure also put it: "In a language there are only differences, without fixed terms."

STRUCTURALISTS

Saussure inspired the structuralist critics of the 1960s, particularly in France, who began to investigate philosophy as one form of "discourse" among others. Every discourse shares a sign system in which the key structural feature is the code of **binary opposites**. For instance, the concept "soul" derives its signification from its opposite, "body", or "light" from "dark", "natural" from "cultural", and so on. The anthropologist **Claude Lévi-Strauss** (b. 1908) maintained that a system of binary codes operates in all cultures as their common logic.

A STUDY OF THE STRUCTURES OF SIGN SYSTEMS WILL EVENTUALLY PROVE TO BE A SCIENTIFIC STUDY OF THE HUMAN MIND.

Structuralists saw the world organized into interlocking systems, allied to genetic "deep structures", with their own "grammars" open to analysis. This view was overthrown in the late 1960s by the "post-structuralists", **Roland Barthes** (1915-80), **Julia Kristeva** (b. 1941) and especially **Jacques Derrida** (b. 1930).

SUPPOSE YOU PUSH SAUSSURE'S INSIGHT INTO THE "ARBITRARY" NATURE OF SIGNS TO THE EXTREME ...

WHAT YOU WILL FIND IS AN "INFINITE PLAY OF SIGNIFIERS" WITH NO DISCOVERABLE ULTIMATE TRUTH.

BECAUSE SIGNIFIERS CAN ALWAYS BE DESTABILIZED BY THEIR OPPOSITES, SIGNIFICATIONS ARE ALWAYS FLUID.

SIGNIFIER

SIGNIFIED

The job of a critic or philosopher is to recognize these "slippages" of meaning and to "read the text against itself".

DERRIDA AND DECONSTRUCTION

The post-structuralist lesson applies to philosophical texts. They too can be read "against themselves", and this is essentially Jacques Derrida's strategy of **deconstruction**. It is not a "method", but more like a therapy in Wittgenstein's sense. It does not seek a "true meaning", a unity, but reveals multiple meanings unconsciously at war with each other in the text. What are exposed as "unconscious" are the binary polarities which underpin metaphysical assumptions.

One element in any binary opposition is always **privileged** over the other …

Man – – Woman

Light – – Dark

Reason – – Emotion

Presence – – Absence

Privileged terms "slip into" the systems that produce social and cultural hierarchies.

LOGOCENTRISM

Deconstruction excavates the internal contradictions and slippages of meaning in a text to remind us that current "meanings" are merely those which are "stabilized" by dominant cultural and political ideologies. For Derrida, the problem is one of "mistaken identity". Philosophers have always assumed that words communicate meanings that are unambiguously present to the mind.

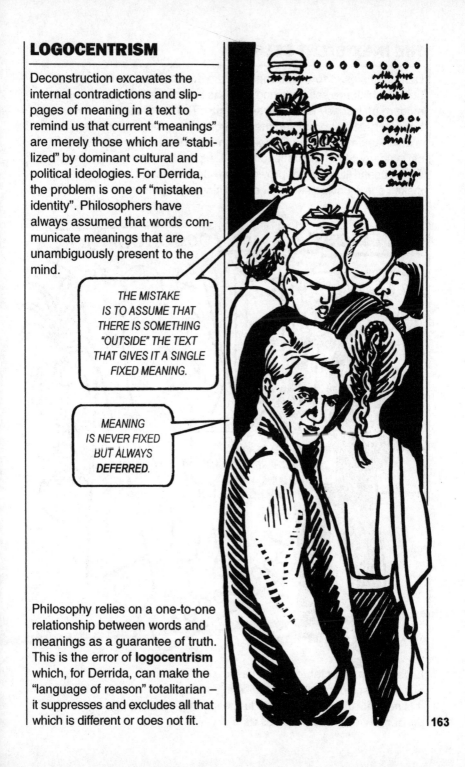

THE MISTAKE IS TO ASSUME THAT THERE IS SOMETHING "OUTSIDE" THE TEXT THAT GIVES IT A SINGLE FIXED MEANING.

MEANING IS NEVER FIXED BUT ALWAYS *DEFERRED*.

Philosophy relies on a one-to-one relationship between words and meanings as a guarantee of truth. This is the error of **logocentrism** which, for Derrida, can make the "language of reason" totalitarian – it suppresses and excludes all that which is different or does not fit.

THE INEXISTENT SELF

Derrida strikes at **foundationalism**: the doctrine that there are basic beliefs which are self-justifying. And the bedrock foundational belief of modern philosophy is Descartes' **cogito**. The psychoanalyst **Jacques Lacan** (1901-81) proposed the disturbing idea that the "self" is a fiction – which undermines the Cartesian and phenomenologists' search for a certainty rooted in a foundational self. A private and unique identity is only a useful illusion that provides us with a sense of security and makes some unified sense of our shifting experiences.

STAR LIGHT NITE CLUB

WHERE I THINK – "I THINK THEREFORE I AM" – THAT IS WHERE I AM NOT.

Lacan claims that the deepest part of us, our unconscious, is structured like a language. It is not until the child acquires language that it enters the social world and becomes an "I".

THE END OF GRAND NARRATIVES

Postmodernism also takes philosophy into the areas of social and political history. In this context, **Jean-François Lyotard** (1924-98) has undermined another crucial "foundational" myth: the idea of **progress** itself, which ever since the Enlightenment had been an applied principle of reason. 20th century modernism had naïvely and disastrously inherited an Enlightenment faith in the "grand narratives" of emancipation, wealth creation and universal truth. Lyotard argues in **The Postmodern Condition** (1979) that these "grand narratives" of a rationally ordered society have collapsed.

WHAT HAS THE MODERNIST BELIEF IN LIBERATION ACTUALLY PRODUCED?

We have endured Fascism, seen the end of Communism, and now witness mafia-style economies, free market greed and environmental disasters on a global scale. If these are the end results of "objective reason", there must be something wrong with it.

FOUCAULT: POWER PLAYS

Michel Foucault (1926-84), another key postmodern thinker, goes even further. In his view, power and knowledge are mutually complicit. Systems of social control have developed together with the human sciences since the 18th century Enlightenment. Philosophy itself has been an accomplice in this "power play" of dominating others by marginalizing them. Foucault borrowed Nietzsche's concept of "genealogy" to carry out his own socio-historical analyses.

OFFICIAL HISTORIES FILTER, SELECT, PRIORITIZE AND EXCLUDE OTHER INTERPRETATIONS.

SO, YOU'RE SAYING THAT HISTORIES OF PHILOSOPHY (INCLUDING THIS BOOK) ONLY SERVE TO LEGITIMIZE MODELS OF "PROGRESS" THAT ARE WHOLLY IDEOLOGICAL.

Institutionalized "knowledge" is the instrument of power that

pathologizes the "mad", "criminal" and "sexually abnormal".

A WORLD OF HYPERREALITY

Postmodernist thinkers value a plurality of viewpoints and constantly challenge all legislating systems. The world they present to us is often one of fragmented, nightmare "hyperreality", as theorized by **Jean Baudrillard** (b. 1929).

> WE EXIST IN A WORLD OF HYPERREAL SIMULACRA – AMONG SIGNS THAT BEAR NO RELATION EVEN TO A PROVISIONAL SURFACE "REALITY".

> WHICH MIGHT EXPLAIN WHY POSTMODERN PHILOSOPHY STRIVES TO APPEAR PLAYFUL, IRONIC AND PARODIC.

Philosophy has become its own satire – hence, its confusing multi-viewpoints which deliberately draw attention to the slipperiness of its own free-floating signs. Not always a clear or fun read! But how can postmodernists escape from the usual paradox facing all sceptics? How can they claim that reason is a "construct" without relying on some minimal form of reason?

167

WHAT ABOUT SCIENCE?

No branch of human knowledge escapes from this radical and corrosive postmodernist relativism. Science and logic are similarly accused of being "constructs" – merely interpretations of experience. There is no timeless and universal reality, and no certain knowledge of it either.

"SCIENTIFIC" AND "LOGICAL" REALITY IS CONSTRUCTED BY LANGUAGE, AND THERE ARE MANY DIFFERENT CONSTRUCTIONS POSSIBLE

Most modern scientists are now sensibly evasive when asked about the scientific "truth", because they recognize that scientific knowledge is always provisional. Many would admit that they no longer believe in a Nature ordered by fixed "laws" discovered by objective human scientists. Einstein's theory of relativity, Bohr's quantum mechanics, and Heisenberg's Uncertainty Principle all make the role of the **observer** central to scientific knowledge. And if Kuhn is right, scientists are more like religious believers than neutral investigators, and their science is mediated by the rarely questioned central "paradigms" of their community. This is the relativist viewpoint, but there is another …

THE REALIST VIEWPOINT

But not all scientists or philosophers are convinced by postmodernist scepticism. Many would still utterly reject the view that the scientific knowledge produced by the "hard" physical sciences is just "one discourse among others" or a "social construct" relative to a specific Western "world view".

GOOD SCIENCE IS A RIGOROUS AND DISCIPLINED STUDY OF HOW NATURE WORKS. THIS IS REAL.

IT IS PRODUCED BY SCIENTISTS WHO TAKE ELABORATE PRECAUTIONS AGAINST SELF-DECEPTION OR PREJUDICE. AND THIS IS REAL.

Experimental methods have undeniably delivered the goods in cosmology, genetics and much else. Miles, seconds and the act of measuring may be "social constructs", but the speed of light is a very real scientific fact that stays at a stubborn 186,282.34 miles-per-second, is independent of who knows it, and won't go away!

Watch This Space!

WESTERN PHILOSOPHY AT A GLANCE

LOGIC, LANGUAGE, MEANING and THOUGHT

PARMENIDES
THE IMPORTANCE OF REASON

ARISTOTLE
DEDUCTIVE LOGIC

ABELARD
NOMINALISM and UNIVERSALS

HEGEL THE DIALECTIC

ANALYTIC PHILOSOPHY

FREGE, RUSSELL
SYMBOLIC LOGIC and MATHEMATICS

MEANING and REFERENCE

LOGICAL ATOMISM

LOGICAL POSITIVISM
MEANING DERIVED FROM TESTABILITY

WITTGENSTEIN
LANGUAGE BEWITCHMENT
LANGUAGE GAMES

AUSTIN
ORDINARY LANGUAGE.
SPEECH ACTS

C.S. PEIRCE
SEMIOTICS

STRUCTURALISTS
LEVI-STRAUSS

POST-STRUCTURALISTS
BARTHES

DECONSTRUCTION
DERRIDA
LOSS OF CONFIDENCE IN THE POSSIBILITY OF AN OBJECTIVE or PERFECT LOGICAL LANGUAGE

RELATIVISM

SCEPTICISM...

EPISTEMOLOGY - WHAT CAN WE KNOW AND WITH WHAT DEGREE OF CERTAINTY?

EMPIRICAL KNOWLEDGE OF THE "EXTERNAL" WORLD

PLATO
THIRD RATE COPIES, UNRELIABLE

ARISTOTLE
OBSERVATION and INDUCTION

FRANCIS BACON
INDUCTION and SCIENCE

DESCARTES
THE SENSES UNRELIABLE

BRITISH EMPIRICISTS

LOCKE
PRIMARY and SECONDARY QUALITIES

BERKELEY
NO "EXTERNAL" WORLD (IDEALISM)

HUME
OUR "KNOWLEDGE" MORE PSYCHOLOGICAL THAN LOGICAL

"A PRIORI" KNOWLEDGE OF CONCEPTS, THOUGHTS, MINDS

PLATO
MATHEMATICS
THE FORMS
INNATISM
CERTAINTY

DESCARTES
THE CERTAINTY OF CONSCIOUS THOUGHT

MATHS and GOD

KANT
TRANSCENDENTAL IDEALISM:
OUR EXPERIENCE OF THE WORLD IS CONSTITUTED BY OUR INBUILT CONCEPTUAL APPARATUS

HEGEL
HUMAN KNOWLEDGE WILL ALWAYS BE DYNAMIC, HISTORICAL

AMERICAN PRAGMATISM

PEIRCE, JAMES, DEWEY
KNOWLEDGE MUST HAVE "CASH VALUE"

PHILOSOPHY OF SCIENCE

POPPER FALSIFICATIONISM

KUHN PARADIGMS

FEYERABEND
AGAINST METHOD

PHENOMENOLOGY

BRENTANO, HUSSERL
INVESTIGATION OF CONSCIOUSNESS

HEIDEGGER, SARTRE
THERE'S MORE TO BEING HUMAN THAN CONSCIOUSNESS

... BUT IT'S ALWAYS BEEN AROUND SINCE THE GREEKS

METAPHYSICS, SPACE and TIME, CAUSATION, APPEARANCE and REALITY, GOD

PRESOCRATIC PHILOSOPHERS
HOW IS THE UNIVERSE CONSTITUTED?

WATER? AIR? FIRE? MATHS? ATOMS?

PLATO THE "FORMS"

ARISTOTLE FINAL CAUSES

CHURCH FATHERS and SCHOLASTICISM
CAN GOD'S EXISTENCE BE PROVED?

DESCARTES
DUALISM - MIND/MATTER

SPINOZA
MONISM - ONE SUBSTANCE

LEIBNIZ
MONADOLOGY - MONADIC SUBSTANCES

BERKELEY IDEALISM

KANT
PHENOMENAL and NOUMENAL WORLDS

HEGEL
DIALECTICAL IDEALISM

rejected by
  FEUERBACH
  RADICAL MATERIALISM
  MARX DIALECTICAL MATERIALISM

LOGICAL POSITIVISM
METAPHYSICS IS "NONSENSE"

WITTGENSTEIN
"OF WHAT WE CANNOT SPEAK, THEREOF WE SHOULD REMAIN SILENT"

PYRRHO, DIOGENES, SEXTUS EMPIRICUS

DESCARTES
CARTESIAN DOUBT

HUME
ON INDUCTION, CAUSE, ETHICAL "KNOWLEDGE", THE SELF

ETHICS

SOPHISTS
RELATIVISM
CONTRACT THEORY

SOCRATES
VIRTUE IS KNOWLEDGE

PLATO
"THE GOOD" and MORAL EXPERTS

ARISTOTLE
EPICUREANS and STOICS
MORALITY A PRACTICAL SKILL

CHRISTIAN THEOLOGY
DIVINE COMMAND

HUME
IS/OUGHT "GAP": THERE CAN BE NO MORAL "FACTS"

KANT
DEONTOLOGY: DUTIES DERIVED FROM REASON

UTILITARIANS
PUBLIC HAPPINESS

SARTRE
INDIVIDUAL CHOICE and RESPONSIBILITY

NIETZSCHE
LANGUAGE IS METAPHORICAL, THE "TRUTH" UNATTAINABLE

WITTGENSTEIN
PHILOSOPHY JUST ONE LANGUAGE GAME

POLITICS, HUMAN NATURE, AUTHORITY and RIGHTS

PLATO
BENIGN DICTATORSHIP

ARISTOTLE
DEMOCRACY, PLUS SLAVERY

MACHIAVELLI
RUTHLESS RULERS

HOBBES
CONTRACT THEORY

ROUSSEAU
THE GENERAL WILL

HEGEL
THE PRUSSIAN STATE

MARX
THE DIALECTICAL STRUGGLE

GRAMSCI, MARCUSE, FOUCAULT
STATE IDEOLOGICAL POWER

POSTMODERNISM

LANGUAGE
A SELF-CONTAINED, ARBITRARY SYSTEM OF SIGNS WHOSE RELATIONSHIP TO "THE TRUTH" IS DOUBTFUL

LYOTARD
HOSTILITY TO THE ENLIGHTENMENT'S WORSHIP OF "REASON"

DERRIDA
DECONSTRUCTION

LACAN
THE FICTION OF SELF

FOUCAULT
KNOWLEDGE and POWER

BUT - PERHAPS THERE ARE SOME OBJECTIVE TRUTHS THAT ARE NOT MERE "SOCIAL COSTRUCTS"

FURTHER READING

There is a glaring omission of women philosophers in this book. Until recently, women were deliberately excluded from the privileged male domain of professional philosophy. Now there are so many very good ones that it poses a problem of space in a short book like this. Icon's forthcoming *Postfeminism* will remedy this problem, but meanwhile readers might wish to consult some of the key figures: Mary Wollstonecraft, Simone de Beauvoir, Hannah Arendt, Mary Warnock, Mary Midgley, Iris Murdoch, Phillipa Foot, Elizabeth Anscombe, Julia Kristeva and Martha Nussbaum, among others.

Here is a list of books that should be clear and helpful, beginning with some introductions to the history of Western philosophy.

History of Western Philosophy, Bertrand Russell, Routledge, London and New York 1991. Amusing and accessible, but idiosyncratic and now rather old.
A Short History of Philosophy, Robert C. Solomon and Kathleen M. Higgins, Oxford University Press, Oxford and New York 1996. A very thorough and readable guide. It makes a stab at including philosophies other than those of the Western world, but is hostile to most postmodernist thought.
From Descartes to Wittgenstein, Roger Scruton, Routledge, London and New York 1981. Sometimes quite difficult, but does miraculously make the philosophies of both Hegel and Frege accessible.
A History of Western Philosophy, D.W. Hamlyn, Penguin, London and New York 1988. A very thorough and sensible, but sometimes quite demanding, guide to the ideas and arguments of key Western philosophers.
Sophie's World, Jostein Gaarder, Phoenix House, New York 1995, is "a history of philosophy that thinks it's a novel". It's a better history than novel, though.

Individual books in the Oxford University Press **Modern Masters** series are usually excellent on the lives and central ideas of individual philosophers. The one on **Hegel** by Peter Singer is extremely good. Readers who want clear, brief and accessible guides will benefit from the **Introducing** series of classical and postmodern philosophers, of which this book forms a part.

And there are many other useful guides to philosophy, for example:
Philosophy Made Simple, R.H. Popkin and A. Stroll, London, Heinemann, 1986 and Made Simple Paperbacks, New York, 1993.
Introduction to Philosophy, W.J. Earle, Mcgraw Hill, New York, 1992.
Philosophy or Sophia, Brenda Almond, Penguin, London and New York 1988.
Man is the Measure, Reuben Abel, The Free Press (Macmillan), London and New York 1997.
The Philosopher's Habitat, Lawrence Goldstein, Routledge, London and New York 1990.
Confessions of a Philosopher: A Journey Through Western Philosophy, Bryan Magee, Random House, London and New York 1998.

Most philosophy students have been rescued at one time or another by **An Introduction to Philosophical Analysis**, John Hospers, Routledge, London and New York 1990, a book which is more fun than its title suggests
An Introduction to Western Philosophy, Anthony Flew, Thames and Hudson, London 1971. This is a *very good book* because Flew bullies you into thinking for yourself, and so gets you to understand many key philosophical ideas and arguments. Available via Amazon on the Internet.

The Great Philosophers, Bryan Magee, Oxford University Press, Oxford and New York 1988, is accessible because it consists of a series of dialogues between Magee and some modern philosophers discussing key Western philosophers of the past. Magee makes his guests explain things clearly, most of the time.

Issues in Philosophy, Calvin Pinchin, Macmillan, London, and Barnes and Noble, New York 1990, is a good book for anyone foolish enough to think they'd like to study for an 'A' Level or equivalent in philosophy.

The Concise Encyclopedia of Western Philosophy and Philosophers, ed. J.O. Urmson and Jonathan Rée, Unwin Hyman, London 1976, is full of short and lucid articles about major Western philosophers and ideas.

The Oxford Companion to Philosophy, ed. Ted Honderich, Oxford University Press, Oxford and New York 1995, is very thorough and invaluable for when you want to find out yet more about the Achilles paradox or the man who invented it, Zeno. It also shows you what some modern philosophers look like.

ACKNOWLEDGEMENTS

The author is indebted to his incisive and painstaking editor, Richard Appignanesi, the busiest person in the world, and Duncan Heath, the patient and faultless copy-editor of this book. He realizes that, without the intelligence, skill and wit of Judy Groves, this book would probably have been rather dull. He is also very grateful for the patience and understanding of Judith Robinson who thinks that he should get out of his study more often.

The artist would like to thank Howard Peters, Howard Selina, David King and Bill Mayblin for their help with picture research and technical advice. A special thanks to Oscar Zarate for his generous help and to Arabella Anderson who agreed to be photographed for this book.

Dave Robinson has taught philosophy to students for many years. He has recently written and illustrated *Leading Questions*, a book about postmodernist literary theory. He is also the author of *Introducing Ethics* and *Descartes*.

Judy Groves is an artist, illustrator and designer. She has also illustrated introductory guides to Jesus, Wittgenstein, Lacan, Chomsky and Lévi-Strauss in this series.

INDEX